"A spiritual quest that is poignant ar
discovers, is a function of risk and de ... of place."

—Hope Edelman, *Chicago Tribune*

"Morris forgoes satire for wry suspension of disbelief, discovering common ground between her own flight to California and her subjects' eccentric, earnest quests for a more meaningful life."

—Megan Harlan, *Entertainment Weekly*

"Her wry observations of a woman traveling alone with a child are serious, yet her writing is lighthearted, tinged with hope."

—Fred Klein, *Santa Barbara News-Press*

"An engaging memoir of crisis...A frank and open-eyed look at Morris coming to terms with a difficult period in her life."

—Robert Allen Papinchak, *The Seattle Times*

"Her sentences pierce through to capture a situation or a mood, not wasting a single adjective or adverb. At the same time, she can tug at your arm with a gracefully sensuous description."

—Rob Pegoraro, *The Washington Post Book World*

"This is quiet writing, with an almost covert elegance, that evokes the solitude of single motherhood without lapsing into melodrama."

—Claire Dederer, *Seattle Weekly*

"With wry humor and surprising affection, [Mary Morris creates] a vision of Southern California that's both oddly familiar and bracingly strange."

—Valerie Takahama, *The Denver Post*

"A thorough researcher and an engaging storyteller, Morris's accounts of the spiritual movements, leaders, and believers that she encounters are lively, fascinating, and often very funny."

—Jean Patterson, *The Orlando Sentinel*

Also by Mary Morris

FICTION

Vanishing Animals

Crossroads

The Bus of Dreams

The Waiting Room

The Night Sky

House Arrest

The Lifeguard

NONFICTION

Nothing to Declare: Memoirs of a Woman Traveling Alone

Wall to Wall: From Beijing to Berlin by Rail

Maiden Voyages: Writings of Women Travelers

Angels & Aliens

A JOURNEY WEST

Mary Morris

PICADOR USA / NEW YORK

Note to the reader:

The names used for the individuals identified as "Alice," "Angie," "Dr. Henry Z. Chesler," "Eric," "Evan," "Ginger," "Jenelle," "Jeremy," "Jimmy," "Wanda Joy," "Sam Lauderstein," "Laura," "Robin," "Sally Schneider," "Ted Schneider," and "Willa" are not those individuals' real names.

For information on Picador USA Reading Group Guides, as well as ordering, please contact the Trade Marketing department at St. Martin's Press.
Phone: 1-800-221-7945 extension 763
Fax: 212-677-7456
E-mail: trademarketing@stmartins.com

Book design by Gretchen Achilles

Library of Congress Cataloging-in-Publication Data
Morris, Mary.
Angels & aliens : a journey west / by Mary Morris.
p. cm.
ISBN 0-312-19949-X (hc)
ISBN 0-312-20429-9 (pbk)
1. Morris, Mary—Journeys—California. 2. Women novelists, American—20th century—Biography. 3. Single mothers—California—Biography. 4. California—Description and travel. I. Title.
PS3563.O87445Z465 1999
813'.54—dc21 98-43015
[b] CIP

First Picador USA Paperback Edition: January 2000

10 9 8 7 6 5 4 3 2 1

To John Harbison, who sent me into the desert,

to Larry O'Connor, who found me there,

and to Leslie Ernst, wherever she may be

Contents

Main Beach

One

From the window of the plane I follow roads that zigzag through the middle of nowhere. I try to imagine where they are heading. Below me a desert stretches, red and cracked. As we fly across the country, I watch the east recede. When we crossed the Mississippi, childhood slipped away. I am a grown-up now, with grown-up concerns. My daughter, Kate, sits on my lap, her face pressed to the window. My arms ache from holding her.

It is mainly a flight of businessmen, and the man beside me has been working since we got on this plane. When he first saw that he was sitting next to a woman with a baby, he said, "They should have special seating for you." Then he looked away, turning to his papers. I wish I could turn to mine. I've always worked well on trains and planes, in motion. But we are crammed in here.

I point to the clouds. What do you see? Dinosaurs, a rabbit, Superman? My eyes follow the roads, searching for towns, a house, someplace where they go. There is so much space, so much room in between. Lonely houses stand on hills. Nothing can grow here. We may as well be flying over the moon.

As I left the East Coast, my brother pressed a book into my hands. A longtime science fiction buff, he wanted to convince me that I cannot teach literature, or writing for that matter, if I am not familiar with this remarkable genre. On the plane to Orange County, as the baby dozes in my arms, I read *The Martian Chronicles* by Ray Bradbury—a former Midwesterner like myself, who also moved to Southern California.

I read these words: "We've got to forget Earth and how things were. We've got to look at what we have here and how different it is. I get a hell of a lot of fun out of just the weather. . . . It's Martian weather. Hot as hell daytime, cold as hell nights. I get a kick out of the different flowers and different rain. I came to Mars to retire and I wanted to retire in a place where everything is different."

That is what I want as well. A place where everything is different from what has been. Where I can forget what needs to be forgotten and begin again. Yet as the plane circles to land, suddenly I am not so certain. My mother's words from decades ago come back to haunt me. "You take yourself with you," she said in 1967 as she put me aboard the SS *France.* And, of course, she was right.

At the airport, people mill about, smiling, in pastel shirts and khaki trousers, with rehearsed casualness. Everyone seems willing to help. A man in shorts carries one of my bags. "You'll be okay?" he asks.

I blink, fighting back tears. Then I find myself, weeping, in the shadow of John Wayne. The Duke looms above me in his ten-gallon hat, boots with spurs. His statue at John Wayne International Airport where I have landed seems affable enough, relaxed and friendly, but looks can be deceiving, I tell myself, as I peer at the gun and holster strapped to his side. I have sought shade for my baby and me beneath the blinding noonday sun. "Are you all right?" the man in shorts asks again. Clutching the baby in one arm and my typewriter in the other, I nod, knowing I've made the mistake of my life.

My car, which has crossed the country thanks to a friend, is parked in the long-term lot. Squinting in the brightness, I fumble in my wallet until I find the ticket stub and the map that indicates where the car has been parked. Then I push Kate and our luggage on a cart across the burning asphalt and locate my Volkswagen, baking in the sun. All the other cars have cardboard sunshades, designed as sunglasses, palm trees, a bathing beauty. I make a mental note to buy one of these (I never do). Opening the doors, I let the breeze blow in.

When it is cool enough, I drive through this land of perfect climate and giant trees, of huge red hibiscus and purple bougainvillea, to my house at the base of what was once the great Irvine Ranch. I rented this house last winter, thinking I'd be living in it with Kate's father. Now I am here alone. Standing on the patio of my bungalow, I peer down at the ocean. To my left a hawk glides over Boat Canyon—a narrow wedge of a canyon where a few shops reside. Taking a deep breath, I can smell the sea.

The key is under the mat, where my landlord said it would be. When we walk in, the rooms are stuffy. No one has been inside for a long time. I open the windows, and the wind blows right through. By evening the temperature has dropped and we are almost unpacked.

I spend my first night with Kate in that cool house, swept with ocean breezes and the scent of jasmine. My daughter refuses to sleep in her crib and will rest only in my arms. Awake in the light of the blue moon, I listen to the howling of the coyotes that roam the hills above my house. A neighbor has a deep bronchial cough. Somebody's wind chimes jangle in the breeze.

In the morning I wake to a stream of relentless sun. Outside, my neighbor (a woman I will never meet), dressed in a string bikini, zinc oxide on her nose, wears a cordless Walkman that projects two antennae from her head, and I know that I have come to Mars.

• • •

I try to settle in. At the bank, I open a new account, and they give me seashell checks. At a pharmacy, I buy sunscreen and sunglasses in the shape of dolphins for Kate. We head down to Main Beach, where surfers ride the waves and continuous volleyball seems to be in play. Kate and I pause to watch. Bodies slick and muscled slam the ball into the sand. Overhead, a plane flies, dragging a sky ad that reads: JEAN, WILL YOU MARRY ME? LOVE, DOUG. I scan the beach, looking for Jean, elated, clapping her hands. Or perhaps humiliated, turning away.

My car needs minor repairs. An oil check, a windshield wiper replaced. The wiper on the driver's side has been a problem since I got the car. For some reason it flips out of alignment and wipes the side of the car. In the yellow pages I find Ralph's VW shop, which is on Canyon Road, and we drive out there, twisting through the dry, golden-brown hills that line the road.

Ralph, a gentle man with rheumy blue eyes, says he'll take care of my car while I'm living here. He has a son who stands off to the side, holding his father's tools, as Ralph cleans the oil filter, replaces the arm of the windshield wiper. "You won't have a problem with it now," he says, patting the hood. Ralph watches as I make the tricky turn back onto Canyon Road, and the boy stands behind my car, waving until we're gone. Even after we are well on our way, I still see Ralph's son in the rearview mirror, waving.

Kate and I return to Main Beach, where young men in Day-Glo shorts spike a volleyball and someone taps out a tune on his surfboard. We head to the sandbox. It is huge, with dozens of mothers and kids, and I tell myself it might be a good place to meet people.

As Kate is playing, tossing her head of russet curls, she lifts up a little boy's truck, spins its wheels. The mother taps Kate on the arm. "Excuse me, honey," the woman says, pointing a finger at my eight-month-old child, "but that's our toy."

Scooping Kate up in my arms, I carry her along the beach until we come upon a wedding in progress. A bride and groom are exchanging vows on the sand. Beside them is a rocky cliff with a sign that reads: HAZARDOUS AREA. DO NOT CROSS.

Two

There is an ancient map of California that shows it to be an island, floating off the mainland. This island is dotted with ruthless pirates, buried treasure, fistfuls of gold. Indeed, California seems to be as distinct a world as the Galápagos, with species all its own. The entrepreneurs, sun seekers, and believers who made their way here were caught up in a dream of El Dorado. Myself included. Yet others have been less enthusiastic.

Thornton Wilder, a usually upbeat man, while dining one night in Los Angeles with Helen Hayes and her husband, Charles MacArthur, turned to them and said, "You know, one day someone is going to approach this area and it will be entirely desert. . . . There will be nothing left standing. . . . God never meant man to live here."

Evelyn Waugh thought so too. In his essay "Death in Hollywood," he writes: "In a thousand years or so, when the first archaeologists from beyond the date line unload their boat on the sands of Southern California, they will find much the same scene as confronted the Franciscan missionaries. A dry landscape will extend from the ocean to the mountains."

The prospect of calamity is everywhere: in the earth that rattles, the fires that sweep down from the hills, the rains that follow and bring mud and debris flows that carry million-dollar homes from Malibu into the canyons below. Just miles out in the Pacific, El Niño poses a recurring threat. The motto of this state is "Eureka: I have found it." But found what? I wonder as I stand on my patio not long after my arrival, looking out to sea.

From the patio, I am struck by the quality of the light, by its clarity and harsh glare. My sensitive blue eyes are fixed in a permanent squint. I'll wear sunglasses the whole time I'm here. I'm almost blinded by the light; but not quite.

I, too, have come for a fresh start. It seemed when I left New York that I had good reason to do that. I had to get away. I also needed a job, and there was one I could have at a university here. Now I'm not so sure. There is a great tradition of people who moved to California to start over. A whole body of literature is dedicated to this theme, books such as *The Grapes of Wrath* or *The Day of the Locust.* A deluded Grandpa Joad said, "Got a feelin' it will make a new fella out of me." Obviously he was wrong. Just another one of the wishful dreamers. Still you can see the nameless hordes coming to California to pick fruit or be discovered or find a cure for whatever ails them, or, as in my case, to begin again.

Another interesting motif runs through California literature: deaths on the Pacific Coast Highway—car crashes, vehicles sailing over the edge. In the words of Nathanael West, there are people who "have come to California to die," which in fact he did, in relative obscurity, in a fiery car crash. There is, after all, no place to go. Even as I moved here I knew. It's the end of the line.

• • •

The weekend before I left Manhattan, my sublettor needed to move in. He is a friend and remains a friend, so I wanted to accommodate him, but Kate and I had nowhere to go for four nights. I had planned to go to Jeremy's, but he had a conference somewhere in Europe, a case to present at The Hague. I could go there anyway, but what would be the point, rambling with the baby through that big, disorderly house?

In most ways, I am here because of him. A part of me is grateful because I have the child and I have a job, and a part of me is something else, which I haven't quite given a name to yet. When Jeremy was offered a distinguished professorship at Irvine, he said he'd accept if they would create a job for me. So they did.

I was five months pregnant and in the last semester of my job at the university where we'd met. We came out for our interview the winter before Kate was born, and all I remember is that the roads twisted and turned and I could never figure out where I was. The cul-de-sac developments all looked the same. We drove over many speed bumps. I didn't like having to slow down, then go over a bump.

"I want to live near the sea," I told Jeremy as we drove through one planned community after another. We would sell the house in New Jersey where he'd lived with his previous family. Start life anew.

We had not married. I assumed that we would after the baby was born. We had been together five years. I had seen him through his divorce. But he was ambivalent about marrying again. He was older than I by almost twenty years, and he had so many responsibilities. His boys were a problem. His ex had taken a chunk out of him. "I don't want your money," I said. "I just want to be with you."

Ultimately, he turned down the professorship in California. But I hadn't applied for any other jobs. I didn't even know that my job was a deal cooked up by the administration, nothing that made the English Department very happy. But even if I'd known, there was nothing I would have done about it. I had nowhere else to go.

That weekend before I moved to California, I packed a bag of overnight things and roamed the city, staying on a friend's sofa one night, in a maid's room in a basement another. During the days, I wandered, pushing the stroller in and out of air-conditioned museums, movie theaters. Keys were left for me in one place; other friends, heading off to dinner, let me in before they went out.

The night we slept in the maid's room, Kate pressed to the wall beside me in a cot, I knew my time in New York was over. On Monday morning I went back to my apartment to collect our bags, all neatly packed and waiting at the side of the living room. I paid a few bills, tidied up my affairs, and then, as if it had never been our home, we were gone.

There is a man named Stan who takes care of the bungalow I have rented from the nice family who went to Ireland for the year. He has a BEAM ME UP, JESUS bumper sticker on the back of his Jeep. Stan and his wife, Kathy, live in the studio attached to my bungalow. On the patio, there is a small sandbox, whose contents his cat uses as litter, and for the year I am living there he keeps promising to put a lid on it. The patio is filled with lumber, because Stan is building a back porch. He is almost deaf, which I don't realize until Kathy tells me. Indeed, when I told Stan the faucet dripped, he had said, "I don't hear a thing."

Our neighbors are a couple with two boys, and they seem

willing to share child care. I made this arrangement, sight unseen, before leaving New York. They have a Mormon baby-sitter, Jenelle, who is about twenty years old and humorless. She wears a big engagement ring on her finger, and purple eyeliner is spread thickly across her lids. The TV is always on when I go to drop Kate off. I pay only two-fifty an hour, which is all I can afford, so I shouldn't complain, but still I do.

I ask her to keep the TV off and play with the kids. "Oh, I take them to the beach," she says. In fact, my neighbor, Monica, and I have purchased a double stroller. The older boy, Max, can walk. I do come back to find Kate bronzed, freckles on her nose, but sitting glazed in front of *Sesame Street.*

I try to talk to Monica about this, but it is difficult. She says, "Oh, they just chill out that way." She and her husband, Mike, met on the Pirates of the Caribbean ride at Disneyland when they were fourteen. They have been together ever since. When Monica describes for me how they were thrown together as the ride splashed along, soaking them, pirates shouting, she blushes. He is a waiter at an upscale restaurant in town, but he's writing short stories and screenplays. He says he wants to show them to me, but in all the time I live there, I never see a word he writes.

I drop Kate off in the morning as I head to school. Jenelle plunks her down in front of the TV, promising that they'll be at the beach in no time. I hurry off so I can't hear Kate cry.

At school, they call me their "writer in residence." My students are tall blondes who have domestic tales to tell, Vietnamese with boat stories, Hispanics with the woes of immigration and a hunger for the American dream. Some of my students drive me wild. One in particular. He has a handlebar mustache, wears suspenders and a Fantasy Island pin. He is writing about his own version of Narnia, and he spends long sessions in my office. He brings me maps, executed in minute detail, explaining how his kingdom works, underground tunnels where antimatter creatures live like moles. He has a whole theory about life on the other side of mirrors. He believes in elves. Something about him frightens me.

Much of my day is spent driving from one place to another. As I drive, I begin to notice the license plates. One of my neighbors has a plate that reads TOPGUMS. There's an old lady who drives a Mercedes, and hers says FUNFOX. The drivers are pretty aggressive, and I have to do some fancy maneuvering, but I like being in the car, cruising. It is, however, the time of drive-by shootings. Not far from where I live, a young man is shot in the neck, paralyzed from the waist down. His story is front-page news. As I cross lanes casually on the 405, a man points his finger like a gun and pretends to shoot me.

I drive defensively, eyes straight ahead. I keep a pad with me and write down license plates. NJOYMNT, ICRE8, LIVN4NOW, REDE4LV. Another reads MSNLNKH, which I can't figure out. Still, I write it on my pad. I contemplate what my own license plate might read, but nothing seems right.

Even though it is out of my way, I like the stretch of road through Laguna Canyon, the one that takes me past Ralph's VW shop. It is a narrow, beautiful road that seems to twist of its own accord. In 1998, in the season of El Niño, this road will serve as a conduit for mud slides, carrying furniture to the sea, smothering a young man in its wake. But for now, in September, it is redolent with the smell of oranges and, in the spring, strawberries. Already the migrant workers are beginning to prepare its fields. Hawks soar above the hills.

In the evening this canyon road leaves me dizzy. Later I will learn there is a legend about it. The Laguna Indians were angry about this path being carved through their canyon, and so a spirit makes the roadway shift at night, hurling automobiles into the lights of oncoming cars. It is true that this road is infamous for the head-on collisions that happen at night.

Years later, this canyon will burn in the brush fires of the late nineties. I will be flying into Los Angeles, and a firefighter sitting next to me will point out Laguna Canyon, where he's headed. The fire just swept through that canyon, he told me, like someone was chasing it.

Three

Orange County, California, where I am to spend the next year of my life, is said to be the bastion of right-wing America. The Minute Men, the militant branch of the John Birch Society, originated here. Richard Nixon, then reclusive and downtrodden, dwelled in the hills of San Clemente. He once contemplated having his winter White House just above the bungalow I have rented in Laguna Beach.

During World War II, the lower middle classes left the South and the Midwest for Orange County, to take jobs in the defense industry. They had come to California not only for the work but for the space and the weather. In the overcrowded, smoggy developments near the defense plants they found neither. But they had their cars and their swimming pools and, of course, their beliefs.

Here is where born-again religious fundamentalism found its home. Where theme parks and idyllic subdivisions, even if they are inland, abound with names like Mediterranean Breeze or Ocean Shores or Plaza del Sol. It is in Orange County that I am to live for a year in a little bungalow overlooking the Pacific Ocean, a place that most people in this world would envy calling home.

I take up residence in the bungalow that overlooks the sea, but soon a restless pacing begins. When I am not unpacking or driving to my job, I wander these cliffs, up and back like a cougar. From the cliffs I peer down at the beaches they used as the location for the "Forbidden Zone" in the movie *Planet of the Apes.* It was just below my house that the head of the Statue of Liberty lay buried in the sand. What is it that Charlton Heston utters as his spaceship is catapulting toward—where else?—California pretending to be New York? "Time bends. Space seems endless. The human ego is crushed here. I am lonely."

So am I. Every day, as I walk my baby along the cliffs, I think to myself: I could just jump off and end it all here. I have no friends, no one to turn to. The opportunity for becoming a cliché in West Coast fiction is obvious. But as I watch the water battering the rocks, I know that I cannot leave my child behind, because who would care for her? And I can't take her with me, because even in my despair such selfishness is not an option. I have no choice. I have to live. Besides, her father and I have not made a clear decision. Nothing was made final between us. We are apart; that is all.

Every night, Jeremy calls to see how we are. He is a night owl, so he phones at two or three in the morning, his time. It is near midnight where I am. I am the last thing he does, he tells me, before he goes to sleep. Some nights, if he is traveling or attending some function in the city, he doesn't call, and then it is difficult for me to fall asleep. Though I try not to, I keep waiting for the phone to ring.

On weekends especially I wait for his call. Then I get tired of waiting and go for long walks with the baby on the cliffs and come back to find his messages. He'll talk into my tape about politics, his tennis game, something Tolstoy said in the second epilogue to *War and Peace*, us, the weather in New York, how strange it is that I am not nearby, a brief mention of the baby, his squash game. Sometimes he uses up the whole tape.

He seems to have an uncanny ability to call when I am out. When I mention this, he says it's a Zen thing. You need to let go in order to have. You never get what you try to hold on to.

The woman next door stands by the side of the road, a volleyball in her hand. Across the street is her four-year-old daughter. The woman tosses the ball into the street whenever a car comes, then raises a finger, daring her daughter to run after it. The child hesitates, her eyes darting between the ball and her mother's upraised finger.

A truck pulls up. A man knocks on my door. The insignia on his shirt reads TOTAL EXTERMINATING. He has a buzz cut and a brown uniform. Reluctantly I let him in.

On Sunday, I notice, people wash their cars. As I walk Kate in the stroller, I observe this odd ritual: cars foaming with suds, owners slinging buckets of water over them. The one acquaintance I have made at school invites me to a Tupperware party. She tells me she actually likes them. The women get roused to a frenzy. She says there are great incentives. You are given prizes, which are then taken away. Tupperware, she informs me, has a lifetime guarantee.

I say I'll go, but then I call back to tell her I have other plans. The day of the Tupperware party, I wash my car. I do not do it myself but take it to the nearest drive-through car wash. Kate laughs so much as the car goes through the scrubbers that I pay to go through again.

When we get home, I make her dinner, give her a bath. Then we sit on the floor and play peekaboo. It is a game Kate can play for hours. I have papers to grade, work to do, but I entertain her with this game. Whenever I try to stop, she cries until we start again. I've never felt very good at games. I'm good at work but not sure I'm good for play. Still, I try.

I hold a shirt to my face, then come out and startle her. I do this dozens of times. She always laughs, cries if I stop. I'm never sure if I'm doing it right.

I've read once said that creative people, even if they had a happy childhood, tend to remember an unhappy one. I remember rainy days, fried chicken splattering my mother's hand, a party where a magician pulled a rabbit out of a hat while I cried in the other room. I remember crying a lot. Crying at nursery school the day everyone went to see the fire truck, crying into my mother's skirts the first day of kindergarten. She had to pry my fingers away. Then I cried into Miss Malvey's skirts. I wonder why I clung in that way.

When I was a girl on days when there was no school, I walked in the woods. I was a pioneer girl, an Indian squaw, a brave scout. I explored ravines, searching for arrowheads. Climbed down the bluff. I chased butterflies, dressed like a cowgirl. Once, I lay down with my face in the grass, pretending I was dead. I liked the feel of the cool grass on my face, the tingling that went through my limbs. I stayed there until a woman stopped in a car and told me that wasn't a nice thing to do.

I remember not doing things right. Dropping dishes, leaving lights on. I remember shouting, fingers pointing. A long list of rules I had trouble following, like breaking my bread before I buttered it. Putting my napkin in my lap. There was a different way of eating hot soup and cold soup. For one, the spoon moves toward you; for the other, away. I could never get it straight. I remember my father's brown leather slippers, which I'd bring down to him as soon as he walked in the door. In the evening, the TV always on, my father was behind a newspaper.

At night my mother blew good-night kisses from my doorway. She'd call out, "Roses on your pillow," then blow a kiss. "Did you catch it?" she'd ask. My father told me bedtime stories and sang me songs. I couldn't go to bed without this routine. A story, a song, a back rub. Stories about a brook and a bridge, about a woman who lived inside a pumpkin, about the little snowflake. The brook and the bridge was a story about progress and, as I look back, somewhat boring, and the woman inside the pumpkin frightened me. But the little snowflake was a story I made him tell me night after night.

It was about a snowflake who wanted an adventure, so he left his mother and father and his snow cloud and fell to earth. He fell and he fell, and as he fell he noticed thousands and thousands of other snowflakes, which were just like him. When he got to the earth, he landed on a snowdrift where he could see into a house. And in the house he saw a beautiful tree and children opening presents and parents kissing their children. Then he wept for his mother and father and sister and brother snowflakes, for the family he'd left behind. He wept until a bird took pity on him and flew him home. And when the little snowflake got home, he asked his father what that tree was and what the bird was, and of course the tree was a Christmas tree, and the bird was the dove of peace.

We were Jews and this was not a very Jewish story, but it is the story my father made up. It is the one I begged for night after night. This was my father's message to me—that I should stay put. That I should never leave home.

Crystals

Four

My back is bothering me. I assume it is from picking up Kate so much and from all the driving I do. I also suffer from an old injury—a childhood fall from a horse. It all seems compounded now. I try stretches, hot baths, but the pain is socked in. Through Monica next door I get the name of a masseuse named Angie. "She's good and she's cheap," Monica says.

"That's what I want," I tell her.

Angie's office is located in the small strip mall near Newport Beach. Her table is in a big open room with a view of the sea. In the corner of the room, which smells like cedar, a little fountain bubbles, a Buddha sitting in it. A tape of gulls and ocean waves plays. At first I think it is the sea, but then I see the tape deck, the turning tape. As I make my way to the table, I stumble over a circle of polished stones that surrounds it. Angie, a tall, tan woman with frizzy brown hair, is quick to straighten them.

"What's that?" I ask her before we begin.

"Oh, it's just different healing crystals, some pieces of agate." She bends down and picks one up. "This is Apache Tears. It awakens your dormant potential by releasing repressed emotion."

"How does it do that?"

"The stones help reorganize your energy fields. They will balance your light and dark forces."

"But *how* do they do that?"

Angie gives me a little smile, sensing a skeptic on her table. Then she drops some colored stones—pink, a shiny blue, a yellow green—in each of my palms, closes my fists around them. "Each stone has different properties. Each interacts with different impulses in the body." Opening my fists, she checks the stones. "What do you feel?"

I give a shrug, and she wraps my fists firmly around the stones again. Then she rubs her hands together, closes her eyes, and places her hands over my head as if she is saying a prayer. She is giving her energy to me. Angie has a gentle but firm touch, and we talk as she works on me. Her goal is to move my energy around. "It's not just a back rub, you know. I'm a healer."

"I didn't know that," I tell her.

"Well, now you do." There are two kinds of problems with energy in the body, Angie tells me. What you want to do in healing work is remove the toxic and move the static. The toxic is what poisons you; the static is what gets in your way.

The toxic and the static: this makes sense.

Angie digs her hands deep into my flesh. She explains that part of her work is to rearrange the organs.

"I was just hoping for a massage."

"But you have a lot of energy to move." She digs somewhere in the area of my spleen. "You're a little tense, aren't you?"

"A little."

She rubs my liver, my spleen, where she claims a lot of bile is being held in. "You're angry about something, aren't you?" I suck in my cheeks, nod my head slightly.

"Well, you need to relax more."

I decide to get into a good routine. Do some stretches before breakfast, eat grainy foods, lots of fiber. If I'm in California, I may as well do the California thing. I get up earlier to practice a little yoga, make oatmeal, spend more time with Kate. Angie was right; I need to relax more.

One morning I'm starting to feel peaceful as I sit in the rocker, which I've turned so that it faces the sea, and nurse Kate. I do this every morning: nurse her in the rocker. My mother says I should wean her, but Kate is not even a year old. Actually I never wean her. It is only after we are able to sit up and have conversations about when she's going to stop nursing that she makes the decision.

The rocker sits under a ceiling fan, and some days, as the morning sun streams in, I sit looking at the motionless fan and for some reason, staring into its smooth, even blades, find comfort. This morning I am growing drowsy watching the fan, when its blades start to turn. Ever so slowly at first, they are turning nonetheless, then a little faster. The fan's circle grows wider and wider, and soon the light fixture that hangs below it joins in. They spin in an ever-widening orbit, ready to spin out of control.

I think it must be a strong breeze, but it is like no breeze I have ever known. I clutch Kate to me as the floor moves, the walls shift, the hills outside my door roll.

When it stops, I race outside. Stan, my deaf neighbor, is shaking his head. People I've never seen emerge from their homes.

Not the big one, everyone seems to agree. But watch out for the aftershocks.

That evening I call my mother. I am still upset, distraught.

"You can't live alone," my mother says. "Get help."

"What kind of help?"

"Someone to live with you. I'll pay for it," my mother says.

When I lived in Mexico, not so far from where I am now, in 1978, Guadelupe Martínez used to be my neighbor and it occurs to me that perhaps she will come and live with me for a while. I still have the phone number of a friend of a friend in San Miguel, where Lupe used to go for her messages. I call three or four times but get no reply. Then I phone again, and the woman who answers doesn't know the name. "Guadelupe Martínez," I tell her.

"Oh, yes, I remember her, but she died."

"She died!" I cry into the phone. "But that can't be possible." There is rumbling, a shouting noise in the background, and then the woman says, "Oh, no, I guess I made a mistake. That was someone else. Call back later, and my sister can help you."

That evening I call back, and the sister says Lupe has moved to another village, with one of her daughters, but she has no phone. The woman doesn't even know where she is living. She is helping to raise her grandchildren now. I ask the woman if she ever hears from Lupe, and she replies, "Oh, from time to time."

"So can you give her a message? Ask her to call Mary," and I give her my number, assuming that I will never hear from Lupe again.

My mother decides to come out until I get settled. In truth, I think she thinks I'm falling apart. What was I doing, moving out here on my own, with no friends, no family around? Well, I needed a job and I needed to get away from Jeremy. I was circling the wagons, regrouping. Now, however, though it has been only a few weeks, it seems I cannot make it on my own.

Defeated, I pick up my mother at the airport and take her home. She likes my bungalow, thinks it is very sweet. "Light and airy" are her words. "You should have friends over, entertain here."

"Who am I going to have over?" I ask. "I don't know a soul."

"You will; you'll meet people."

She knows I'm in the dumps and suggests we all go out for dinner. We drive down the hill to a Chinese restaurant, where on the menu, in big red letters, it says: "All fish must have reservations in advance." We look at each other, and for the first time in weeks I start to laugh. I laugh until tears come to my eyes, and then I laugh some more.

That night my mother sleeps in the room with Kate. I get up once in the night to nurse the baby, then I put her back to bed. I am asleep at about five A.M. when the bed begins to swirl under me. The whole house shakes like Jell-O, and I think I'm going down in a mud slide. I wake up screaming, stagger into the room where they are sleeping. "Where's the baby? Where's my baby?"

Dazed, my mother shouts back at me, "Shut up, Mary. She's all right."

"Shut up?" I scream at her. "There's an earthquake, and I don't know where my baby is."

My mother points to the crib. "She's there, she's fine. Now go back to sleep."

But I can't go back to sleep. Instead I pace the living room, sit in the rocker. I gaze up at the hillside behind my house, imagining fire, mud, another, more shattering quake making its way here. Where was the epicenter of the last one? I wonder. Wasn't it just a few hundred yards out to sea?

The next day we go to an agency my mother locates in the yellow pages, and I find Ramona there. She is a small Mexican woman whose long skirt hides her feet, which are bare in her sandals. She giggles whenever I speak to her, as if my Spanish is gone, which is somewhat disconcerting. Speaking to her is like speaking to a child. She has a peculiar bald spot on one side of her skull, which is partially covered by her hair.

After we leave the agency, I tell my mother I can't do this. I can't have a stranger living with me. "You have to," my mother says. "You can't do this on your own."

Friends of my mother's from Chicago are visiting L.A. They have hired a limo and want to take us to lunch at the Ritz-Carlton in Laguna Niguel. The Hokins are among my mother's more elegant friends. I've always liked them, but I'm not sure I'm up for a limo and the Ritz-Carlton. In fact, it's about the last thing on earth I want to do, but my mother insists. "They're old friends; they've known you since you were a child."

As we prepare to leave, I hear my mother cursing. "What is it?" I ask her. "What's wrong?"

"I ordered cream crepe, and they sent me sandal taupe." She holds up her stockings.

"Does it matter?" I ask, wondering how such things *could* matter.

"Yes," she says. "It matters to me."

The Hokins pick us up, and the limo driver, named Dusty, opens the door. Dusty has long pink nails, dyed yellow hair. She's tall and a bit broad, kind of a hunk, but she's very nice and fusses over the baby. Mr. Hokin, a debonair man with a shock of white hair, who pretends from time to time that he'd like to run off with me, is chatting with Dusty about real estate. Grace, his wife, is going on about some Hockneys she's just seen.

At the Ritz, tall vases overflow with lilies as blond young men in white starched shirts pour water into tall glasses. A bountiful buffet greets us—chafing dishes of eggs, hash, creamed mushrooms, glazed carrots. Serving platters overflow with shrimp, strawberries, asparagus vinaigrette. I am not even hungry and wish I could slip the food into Ziploc bags, take it home. I am barely making ends meet, wondering how I'm going to afford child care and the house I rent, and I gaze at the buffet of buttery eggs, fresh berries. A leggy blond waitress appears. My mother is a diminutive Jewish woman, whose own mother spit into the air to keep the evil eye away. She takes one look at the waitress and orders gestapo soup.

"Mom." I hit her in the ribs.

"Oh, what is it? Gazpacho. Gestapo. I always make that mistake."

The waitress stares at her, stony-faced.

When we leave the restaurant, Dusty is leaning against the limo, smoking a cigarette. She's got an arm resting on the hood of the car. I take Mr. Hokin aside. "I think Dusty is Dustin," I say to him.

He looks Dusty up and down. "I believe you're right."

My mother leaves after Ramona agrees to come and live with us for two hundred dollars a week, plus room and board, Monday through Friday. It seems like a lot of money to me, but at the airport my mother says, "I'll take care of it." The truth is there is no way I could afford eight hundred dollars a month on my salary. But somehow when I made the pact with my parents—that I was having this child and would be doing it on my own—they said they'd be there for me, and they have been.

I was in Leningrad when I called Jeremy to tell him I was pregnant. We had been traveling together in China, then gone our separate ways. Though I had begged him to accompany me on the Trans-Siberian Railroad through Russia, he left me in Shanghai, heading home. Across Siberia I slept. I lay down on my bunk, watching the Russian woods, and drifted off. When I got to Moscow, I knew. I reached Jeremy in New York, just as he was leaving for a lecture series in New Zealand, and told him I thought I was going to have a child. "Oh," he said. "A child is a wonderful thing."

"I think we should make it legal," I told him.

"Legal in what sense?" he replied. Since he is a renowned professor of international law, I assumed he knew what legal meant.

I was looking at forty, and desperately wanted a child. But the man I'd been with for the past several years didn't want to get married. I didn't think I could do it on my own. In despair, I called my mother to say I was coming home, that I was going to have an abortion, and not to tell my father. She gave me her assurances, made her promises. But two hours later, as I lay in my bed in Leningrad, awake through the white night, the phone rang. "Men come and go," said my father, who had been a bachelor for forty-five years. "A child is forever."

"Can you live with this?" I asked him.

"I can live with a lot worse," he said, though I'm not sure he's ever really had to.

During World War II my father was already too old to be in the army, so he went to Pennsylvania to work in the war industry, manufacturing tanks. He lived in Pennsylvania for four years, and one day near the end of the war, his girlfriend, a divorcée with a young child, who wanted desperately to marry my father, asked him to accompany her to a fortune-teller. My father was no believer, but he agreed to drive his girlfriend down some of the worst streets in Pittsburgh, to where an old woman lived in a basement apartment.

The girlfriend wanted to marry my father and she wanted the fortune-teller to make a prediction, but the old woman had nothing to say to her. Instead she asked to see my father, who was waiting near his car. He went in, and the fortune-teller told him that he would receive a letter from a loved one, asking him to go into business, and he would accept. Through that loved one he would meet a woman and marry and have two children and live in a white house by the lake.

A month later my father received a letter from his youngest brother, Sidney, whom he adored. Sidney couldn't make a go of his architectural business. Would my father come and run it for him? Just as a fortune-teller predicted it, my father returned to Chicago to work with his brother. When my aunt Ruth, Sidney's wife, went into Saks to return a nightgown, the woman who would become my mother waited on her.

Aunt Ruth recognized the redheaded Rosalie Zimbroff. They had gone to grammar school together. Aunt Ruth said to my future mother, "My brother-in-law has just moved back to town. Can I give him your number?" Three months later they were married. Then I was born and later my brother, John. My father was successful in an architectural firm he and his brother started, and after a few years my parents moved to the suburbs. We lived in the white house by the lake for a dozen years.

I loved the house I grew up in. I loved its white walls and wood trim, its sturdy white brick and picket fence. Its green shutters and big lawn. When our house was built, the carpenter brought us the head of a deer he had killed. The deer head was stuffed and put on the wall of the basement playroom. For my whole childhood I played under its glassy stare.

Once, we visited the house when it was being built, according to my father's design. I was very little, but I can remember the smell of sawdust and fresh paint. I stood there as my father, blueprints in hand, examined the structure of our house, patting the beams, trying to shake an archway.

My mother wanted a closet somewhere, and my father stared

at his blueprints, shaking his head. When they weren't looking, I came across a razor blade. I had never seen a razor blade before, and I drew it across my skin, cutting a line along my forearm. Blood flowed down my arm, soaking into the unfinished wood. My parents screamed, horrified, and the bloodstain was ignored and eventually carpeted over. But this thought has always been a comfort; a part of me remains.

Many years later, long after I am an adult and have left home, I am sleeping in my father's bed. He is away, and my mother, who tends to roam the house at night, has assigned me to this place. I wake up early, with a thought in my head that I want to write down, and in search of a pen, I open my father's nightstand drawer. The drawer is stuffed full of papers, and this surprises me, because my father is an orderly man.

Though I am not usually a snoop, I begin to rifle through, unsure of what I expect to find—love letters, secret financial records? Instead I find old magazines, hearing aid batteries, assorted cards, photographs of grandchildren as babies. The magazines are in reverse chronological order, as if no one has dipped into this drawer for decades—*Time,* with Qaddafi on the cover, from 1986; my brother's college graduation program from 1973; *Life* from 1962. There are birthday and Father's Day cards from my brother and me, holiday greetings from people I don't recognize but who must be important to my father, because he has photos of them from over the years.

Then I find the maps. The maps surprise me most, because my father is not a traveler. So why would he keep maps? But there is a small pile of them. They are old and folded poorly, salvaged from the glove compartment of a car we haven't owned in years.

On several of them, thick blue Magic Marker lines begin in Chicago and head east.

I recognize these as AAA maps, on which a route has been drawn for my father. I follow the trace of this line and the black arrow that points the way through Gary, Toledo, Cleveland, through places I have never heard of, then sweeps up along the banks of Lake Erie to Niagara Falls.

Now I know where these maps are taking me as I continue on through Buffalo and Albany, picking up the Mass Pike, to Boston. I remember standing with my parents, all of us in yellow rain slickers, as the falls pounded over our heads; the factory-town dreariness of upstate New York; the bucolic stretches along the turnpike. I sat in the back seat all the way.

This is the map my father used to drive me to college over thirty years ago. He has kept it all these years. There is an arrow pointing the way back to Chicago, but I never followed it. Still, my father has held on to these maps as if he believed they would eventually bring me home.

Five

Afternoons, I hike. Endless walks with the baby on my back, through the hills that rise above my house. What am I doing here? I ask myself. There are mountain lions, coyotes, snakes, in these hills. Tempting fate, I take risks I know I shouldn't. I think I'll run into a wild beast, but I don't. There are also butterflies. Kate calls them "bye-byes."

From the hills I cut over to the cliffs that follow the rocky shore. Strangers say good morning to me. People who don't know me give little nods. I stop an elderly man and ask him the time, a question I don't need the answer to. He looks at his watch, tells me it's a beautiful day to be on a walk. "Cute kid," he says, making a face at Kate that makes her laugh. I want to keep talking, but with a little wave the man moves on. I watch him amble away.

No one who knows me lives nearby. I have no idea how I'm going to make ends meet. Though I order them back, my demons begin to rise. Gazing down the rocky embankment, the sea smashing furiously below, I think again that I could end it all here. Then I feel Kate's hand, resting on my neck. Turning, I see her curls, the color of copper pennies, blown by the wind.

I return home to black smoke pouring out the kitchen window because Ramona left pots burning on the stove. A year later the owner of the house will call and tell me she has found half a dozen of her pots, burned, hidden in the basement. I'll have to send her a check to pay for them.

These California cliffs aren't the first where I've contemplated my demise. There was a bluff at the end of our street, and when I was fourteen I knew how I'd die. I'd fling myself down it as soon as I learned I was going to have a child—which at the time was a very dim possibility. There were boys in my life. We met at dances or just before my piano lessons. Sometimes I snuck out along the eaves of my roof. We'd drive around in their cars or sneak off to a corner of the school gym. In my basement we played spin the bottle.

In public, I was a perfect child. I played the piano, I got straight A's, I spoke French, I was on the pom-pom squad. I also popped my mother's Dexedrine, snuck out. There was a boy with slicked-back hair I met before and after my piano lessons. He could do complex fractions in his head. When he walked into class, wearing only white or black, the girls sighed. He would end up a bum, hopping freights, living in the streets. If my father had known I met this boy before piano, he'd have sent me to boarding school.

I kissed boys in corridors, in their parked cars. If any of this ever led to more, if I ever harbored a deep, dark secret, I'd throw myself off the bluff rather than tell my father. I knew this because my father was difficult to please. Lights left on, garage doors open, drove my father wild. One day our new puppy teethed on the sofa, leaving the upholstery in shreds. I watched my terrified mother on the floor, putting her degree in dress design from the Art Institute of Chicago to good use. Needle in hand, pins in her mouth, she reupholstered the sofa before the 5:10 arrived.

I was not much better than the dog—whimsical, not easily tamed. I couldn't set the table right, I didn't stack the dishes in the dishwasher properly. I couldn't make salad or clean my room. I knew this. I was told it all the time.

One day when I was sixteen and taking a nap, the woman I baby-sat for wanted me to come over. My mother woke me, and I shouted profanities at her, called her names she didn't know I knew. My mother covered her mouth, stood against the wall, expecting me to stab her with the butcher knife she envisioned under my mattress. Who is this person? She wanted to know. I had gone to sleep a child and woken up a monster.

I ran barefoot in the rain, all the way to my friend Phyllis's house. I stayed there for the rest of the day; then after a couple of phone calls, I went home. I ran away a few more times after that. One night I ran to my boyfriend David's house and slept in his twin bed all night. In the morning his mother knocked on the door. "David, Mrs. Morris is on the phone, and she wants to know if you know where Mary is."

"Yes, Mom, I do," David replied matter-of-factly. "She's right here."

In high school the bluff was becoming more and more a possibility. Boys were showing up on my back porch when my parents slept. They drove me to parties, though we rarely got there. Instead we drove down to the lake, drank beer, made out. Senior year, there was a rumor that Sally Schneider, whose father played cards with my father, was pregnant, and soon it was more than a rumor, because her father, Ted, threw Sally out of the house.

We lived in a suburban town of nice, big houses and families who didn't throw their daughters onto the street. Sally, we heard, went to live with her boyfriend's family. Other girls puffed up, disappeared for a while, came back thin. But Sally wasn't going to give her baby away.

One day I picked up the phone extension and heard my father on the line. He was speaking in a loud, firm voice, and I knew after a few moments that the man he was talking to was Ted Schneider. I heard my father say, "If Mary ever got into trouble, she could always come home. We'd never turn her away."

Gently I put the receiver down. After that the bluff became the place where I walked, where I rested my back against the tree bent in the wind, where I went to contemplate my fate, not my demise. I tried to be a good girl. I really did. For years I tried to be what everyone wanted me to be, whatever that was. Jeremy was the end of a long string of efforts, attempts that failed.

But one thing is certain. They never turned me away.

• • •

I teach fiction writing in a trailer that serves as a temporary classroom across a pedestrian mall from my office. Either the trailer is very hot or the air conditioner clangs. There are too many chairs in the room, and we cannot put ourselves in a circle. My students tend to sit in the back rows, as far as they can be from me and still be in the classroom. My Fantasy Island student with the handlebar mustache sits right next to the door. I have asked them to move forward, but they prefer to make easy exits in the rear. I am adrift in front of the classroom, my students poised to leave.

I try to give the usual assignments. Write a story about a character who is your opposite, whom you then meet in a bar. Write a story based on a newspaper article, write a story based on an object in your room. When it is time to talk about their stories, two of the older women do all the talking. They are both good writers, though one of them writes painful stories about giving birth to a stillborn child. When I suggest that she might need fictive distance from this material, she snaps, "Don't tell me what to write about."

My students for whom English is a second language don't seem to understand a thing. This course is required for them, a substitute for composition, and a few of them doodle or sleep when I am talking. Some write down every word I say. I have asked them not to do this. "This is a workshop," I explain, "not a lecture."

"But we need good grades."

"Then do your work, come to class, participate, and you'll get an A," I tell them, trying to be reassuring, but half of them think this means I have no judgment. The other half give me worried looks. The Vietnamese students in particular are concerned about their grades. Newly arrived, they have plans for careers in business. They want to get ahead. One has asked me to put grades on all his short stories.

"But that isn't something I do," I try to explain.

"I need to know where I stand," he tells me.

My Fantasy Island student rarely speaks. Then one day he turns in a story about a student who believes his teacher has stolen his idea for a novel and publishes it. The book becomes a best-seller, and the student shoots the teacher at the blackboard. I tell the Fantasy Island student that his story makes me uncomfortable.

"I wanted to try something realistic," he says.

At night when I come home from work, I watch TV. This probably wouldn't be strange for most households, but I have never done it before. I sit and stare for hours at *L.A. Law, Hill Street Blues,* murder mysteries, sitcoms, the news; I draw the line at quiz shows. I start to know the story lines, to identify with the characters and their troubles. If I miss an episode or am interrupted, I feel thrown off for days.

Sometimes, with Kate dozing off in my arms, Ramona comes into the room and sits watching TV with me, though I wish she wouldn't. When Ramona looks at me, she giggles. I don't know what it is, but she cannot look at me and not laugh. Everything is funny to her. Later I will realize that this is a nervous laugh, but I find it disturbing, as if she is laughing at me. When she is not giggling, Ramona gazes longingly out the window.

We sit together at dinner and try to make small talk. Then one night over dinner she has that sad look in her eye, and I ask her what is wrong. She tells me that she misses her son.

"Your son? You didn't tell me you had a child."

Ramona looks at me sheepishly. "I thought you wouldn't want me," she says. Andreas is six years old and lives with Ramona's mother in Morelia. "I am like you," she tells me. "There is no father around."

I feel myself grow defensive. Jeremy is around; he's just not here. But I don't want to argue this point with Ramona. On the other hand, Jeremy never signed the affidavit acknowledging his paternity. Because we were not married, the office of birth records required this before I could write something on Kate's birth certificate under "father's name." She went home from the hospital with me in a cab, and that space remained blank.

"Someday," Ramona says, "when I have enough money, I'll bring my son here to live with me." I hold Kate, sniff her milky breath, run my hand across the sweat on her brow. I fought hard to have her; I cannot imagine her living away from me.

Ramona's mother writes from Morelia, and Ramona has a recent letter. She shows me a picture of a beautiful child with dark skin and big black eyes, tells me how he is an honor student in the first grade. When she talks about him, she tugs on the hair she pulls across her bald spot. There is a sadness in her eyes that won't go away.

If I will be late coming home from school, I call and ask Ramona to put the dinner on. One night she puts on the fish, broccoli, and rice all at the same time. The fish cooks for forty-five minutes before I arrive. The broccoli too.

When I try to explain to Ramona that the fish takes less time to cook than the rice, she giggles. It must be my Spanish, I tell myself. Whenever I come home, she has Kate all bathed and ready for bed, her hair neatly combed. She smells sweet as a puppy. I wish someone would take care of me as well.

On weekends, when Ramona leaves to stay with her friends in Santa Ana, I am miserable—lost and alone. Sunday is the worst day. It is the day when I smell chicken on mesquite grills and see picnics down at the beach. Grandmothers push baby carriages past my house. I envision happy families, joking over barbecues and beer.

Usually I call Jeremy. If he is out, I panic. I imagine the worst. I leave desperate messages on his machine, then go somewhere because I can't bear to stay home and wait for his call. Invariably he phones when I am out, pushing Kate on our endless walks along the cliffs, and he leaves long messages about how he was just at the library, how I need to trust him more.

When I get home, often at dusk, I sit listening to these messages and know this is true. I know he is right. Why can't I be more trusting? Why don't I believe? Why can't I be more patient? It doesn't occur to me that I was patient before I met him, so what's the difference now?

I cannot go anywhere without the baby; I can't get any work done. My arms ache from holding her. I wanted this child so much; I wanted her more than anything. This wasn't always the case. In my thirties I wanted a man, a companion, a husband. A child came at the end of that list. I tried to do things in sequence, as most women did. Meet someone after grad school, settle down. See all the movies you want to see. Take all the trips. Be sure to get to Rajasthan. But it hadn't happened that way. The nice men I met weren't appropriate; the appropriate men weren't nice.

Years passed. Friends invited me to their weddings, to their baby showers. I never knew what to get. I'd never registered anywhere, didn't know that mothers liked swings, not toys their babies could swallow. In the end, weddings and showers made me despair. I moved to Mexico, lived there for nearly two years. In Mexico City I almost died of an abscess. The doctors shook their heads when I asked about a child. Nothing is certain, one doctor told me. He'd seen miracles happen before.

When I met Jeremy, I was sure that he was the person I wanted to spend my life with. I began to gaze into baby carriages. I found myself in supermarket lines, playing peekaboo with strangers' children. This isn't like me, I'd tell myself. It's just hormones. But then I wanted it. I wanted a child. My life was incomplete without one. And I wanted Jeremy's child. In China I told Jeremy I wanted to try, and he didn't seem to mind. It happened right away, that fire that coursed through me. On the Yangtze River, I felt her happen to me.

Later Jeremy told me that he didn't think it would be so easy. He knew my medical history. He thought the chances were slim.

Now I have the child, and now, living in California, I find I can barely take care of her, let alone myself. If I drive, it is better. So I drive up and down the freeway. Sometimes I stop at the Irvine Ranch farmers market or at a beach, but I never stay anywhere too long. It is good to get out of the house, but there is nowhere I really want to go.

One Sunday morning I get up early so I can take a shower before Kate wakes. I ease my way out of bed, leaving her sleeping there. Pausing, I wipe the rim of sweat from her brow, smell her breath. She does not stir. I let the shower run until it is steaming hot, then step in. I love the feel of the hot water as it cascades over my skin. My eyes are closed, and I think that this shower is so peaceful. My mind drifts to work I plan to do, places I want to see. I could stay here forever. Then something tells me to open my eyes, and when I do, I see fingers wrapping around the shower curtain.

Kate, who has managed to crawl out of bed and into the

bathroom, flings the curtain back, screaming. She thinks I have left her alone. "I'm right here, darling," I tell her. "I didn't go anywhere." I draw the curtain shut so that water won't get all over, but she pulls it open again. She won't stop screaming until I get out of the shower, curl up wet and naked with her on the floor.

Hour of Power

Six

One weekend a friend, a composer named John Harbison, calls and asks me what I am doing, and I tell him, "Nothing." When he asks how I can be doing nothing, I start to cry. I do this quietly, muffling my sobs, but John hears it in my voice. "Mary, what's wrong with you? I've never seen you this way."

I tell him I don't know, but I seem to be immobilized, paralyzed. He says I should drive out to Reverend Schuller's Hour of Power Crystal Cathedral. I ask him why, and he says, "Because you are in California. Think about fundamentalism, about Elmer Gantry. Think about beliefs."

Belief is something I left behind. I've been a Jew, a Buddhist, a believer, a doubter. But lately I haven't given much thought to any of this. Out in the garden I see Kate, in the blazing sun, playing in the sandbox where the caretaker's cat pees. I can't bear the thought of going to the beach—families picnicking, children playing in the surf. My traveler's instincts are going numb. I have seen only one sliver of California.

Since John was so adamant, I get in the car with Kate and start to drive. I tell myself I am only following orders, but I cannot help being intrigued. To get to the Crystal Cathedral, in Garden Grove, I drive through Santa Ana, along Memory Lane, which follows the dried-up riverbed. The riverbed is filled with garbage, flat tires, discarded auto parts. There is nothing memorable about Memory Lane.

Still, as I arrive, the past comes to me in snatches, things I have left behind. An Illinois road in autumn, horse chestnuts on the ground. The streets of Paris. My New York apartment, where from my first-floor window I watched people walking past. Mexico, where I trod cobbled streets to buy mangoes. I see the faces of friends I've lost track of, others I've outgrown. My family in disparate places. The first trip Jeremy and I took to Tortola, dancing to the conga drums after a blistering day at the beach.

The road winds and turns, and I'm not sure where I am. Everything looks the same, and I'm certain I've been here before. I am going in circles. At last I come to the City. That is what the place where the Crystal Cathedral stands is called. Just the City, as in City of God. To me, New York was always the City, but now I have entered one of a different kind. I take the circular route, looping around until I come to the giant glass-and-steel edifice. A mammoth glass church with thousands of windows, a house you can see through.

I park in the enormous parking lot, and Kate and I wander the grounds. They are sterile, institutional. There is an odd feel here. This appears to be an industrial park, where technocrats work in cubicles, yet everyone is friendly, smiling. Strangers say hello. I feel as if I'm in a scene from *Invasion of the Body Snatchers,* which in fact was set in this part of the world.

We pop into the Book Center of Possibility Thinking. Along with Bibles, they sell special Bible highlighters, Bible bookmarks. Reverend Schuller's books line the shelves. I pick up some leaflets, including a booklet entitled "My Mission, My Ministry, My Methods."

Sitting down at the edge of a small pool, I read how Robert Schuller first came to Garden Grove to preach the word in 1955, with his wife, Arvella. When Schuller tried to set up his ministry, he learned that all the available space had been rented. So as a last resort, he started preaching in a local drive-in theater. That was where his church began. Schuller's first principle is "Find a need and fill it." His second is "Inch by inch, anything's a cinch."

I am struck at first by the use of alliteration. "Here it is, the complete Sunday morning lineup of powerful, positive, possibility-filled programs, and there's a perfect one for you." And when you sign on the dotted line on a piece of beige paper that serves as your membership to the Reformed Church of America, you've agreed to "Worship enthusiastically, work joyfully, witness lovingly, and invest [your] financial support confidently."

Reverend Schuller expatiates, in the face of other TV evangelists, about his salary and expenses and who watches the church coffers and who profits from the donations and where they come from and where it all goes. He's Dale Carnegie for religion. The alliteration serves at least one good purpose: it's easy to remember. Sitting beside the little pool where Kate splashes, I read Reverend Schuller's creed, which in part reads:

When faced with a mountain
I will not quit!
I will keep on striving . . .
and turn the mountain
into a gold mine,
with God's help!
Amen.

The power of positive thinking: I could use a little of this. If only the poetry were better. . . . I've been so bleak, seeing only the dark side. I have lost my faith, my ability to turn the future my way. Now I look up, and I see my daughter beside the small pool, flowers around it. She's got Jeremy's brown eyes, his night-owl ways, but the rest of what I see is mine. If you put our baby pictures side by side, you can't tell us apart. In years to come, we'll eat the same food, wear the same clothes. We'll laugh at the same jokes, be headstrong in the same ways. As I watch her, dipping her hand into the pool, I see myself.

When I was pregnant, I knew she was a boy. I knew because Jeremy had three boys from various unions, so I assumed this would be one as well. I had a name picked out. Jake. I wanted to call her Jake because a friend of mine had a dog named Jake, a black Lab, who walked with me in the hills in South Dakota when I was pregnant. When I walked with Jake, he stayed close to protect me but kept his distance so as not to smother me. I thought these were good traits.

I phoned for my amnio results from a pay phone on a Manhattan street at five o'clock on a Friday. I called and the woman said, "It's a girl." I exclaimed, "Are you sure?" but she'd already slammed the receiver down. I tried to phone back, because I was sure they'd gotten it wrong, but it was five o'clock on Friday, and everyone had gone home. I'll name her Kate, I told myself. After Katharine Hepburn, a woman nobody could push around.

As Kate's fingers splash in the water, I gaze up at the large bronze statue that rests on a small island in the middle of the pool. The inscription reads: "Let him who is without sin cast the first stone." The woman about to be stoned resembles a debutante in a skimpy gown, with a neat little bob and a turned-up nose, nice breasts. Michelle Pfeiffer at seventeen. Christ, who is kneeling, resembles Robert De Niro. The men who contemplate the stoning all have hooked noses, wear long robes, yarmulkes on their heads. One displays scrolls that resemble the Torah.

Taking Kate by the hand, I think I won't be staying long, yet

I am not ready to go home to the solitude of our house by the sea. The sun is hot, and I think that the cathedral might be cool. Besides, there is something irresistibly perverse in me. "Let's visit the cathedral," I say to her as she tries to walk, clasping a finger from each of my hands. I'm still not sure why my friend has sent me here, but I accept it as a kind of mystery, a treasure hunt I must follow. The reason will present itself, I feel sure.

Kate and I stroll the grounds for a few minutes, then wander into the cathedral, where it *is* cooler, and hook up with a tour. Our guide is named Solomon Goodson, right out of Hawthorne. He smiles a broad, toothy grin at his flock, mostly middle-aged couples in pastel leisure suits, and in a dry but dedicated tone offers us the basics. The Crystal Cathedral has more than 10,000 windows of tempered silver-colored glass, which are held in place by a lacelike frame of 16,000 white steel trusses, made for the cathedral. The sanctuary seats 2,890 people. It is 415 feet long, 207 feet wide, and 128 feet high.

As we head inside, Solomon Goodson goes on to speak of the success of Reverend Schuller's ministry. How his church has more than 10,000 members, his TV evangelist message reaches some 1.3 million households. As Goodson continues his memorized speech, I notice that something is happening overhead. Men are rigging wires above me.

Solomon Goodson explains that these men are with Peter Foy Flyers, the same rigging company that flew Mary Martin as Peter Pan, and they are preparing for a rehearsal by the angels for the Christmas pageant, which will begin just after Thanksgiving. "Angels?" I ask, and Goodson smiles at me.

He explains that for every Christmas and Easter, six women train to fly in the church's special pageants. "It's a great honor," Goodson tells us, "to fly with the angels."

As he drones on about the construction of the Philip Johnson cathedral (which the architect considers his masterpiece), about the tens of thousands who come here to worship, I can almost see those angels with silken wings, soaring overhead.

Seven

I have been teaching for a few weeks when the director of my program calls me into his office. His office is darkened, the shades always drawn. A giant wooden owl hovers above his head. Books that surround him in horizontal piles create the feeling of a fortress. At first he is polite, asking me how it is going. Then he mentions, casually, that there have been complaints. Nothing serious, more concerns really. I seem distracted, he tells me. People think I don't like being here.

I don't know at the time (it is all confided to me later, by a friend who teaches in the writing program) that in fact nobody wants me here. They all feel I have been forced upon them, and I suppose I have. They don't care that I have published books, won prizes. They had to take me. And when Jeremy didn't come, nobody could believe that I would.

"It's all new," I tell him. "I'm trying to get my grip on things."

"Well, try harder," he says with a little laugh.

"I need some time," I say.

Now he turns compassionate. He is aware of my circumstances. But, of course, "you've got a job to do," he admonishes me. "Don't let your emotions get in your way."

I leave his office in tears, with nowhere to go. I stop for a coffee at the Irvine Ranch farmers market. As I sip my coffee, it bothers me that the string beans are all arranged by shape and color—yellow, green, and purple. I have a strange desire to mix them up.

In the center of the room, a player piano renders old Jolson tunes, invisible fingers running up and down the keys.

One morning as I'm having breakfast on the patio, I notice that amid the palmettos and bougainvillea, a carved pumpkin has appeared on my neighbor's lawn. The leaves have not turned golden; there's no bite of fall in the air. Nothing has changed since I got here, yet this jack-o'-lantern tells me that the season has changed.

I am invited to a Halloween party at the house of one of the faculty members. A few Halloweens ago, I am told, he came as an SS officer. This year he is dressed as a swashbuckler, complete with eye patch and sword. Beige metal folding chairs are arranged in a circle, and a few people I know from the department are sitting on them.

I am handed a Dixie cup with Chablis from a jug, but just as I take my first sip of wine, two of his students arrive, dressed as Hitler and Eva Braun: He wears a cap and a Hitler mustache. She is dressed in camouflage gear and high boots. They remain standing, repeating the Sieg-heil salute. Everyone thinks this is a great joke, but I feel sick in the pit of my stomach.

I stay for about an hour, then make my excuses to leave. As I drive back to my bungalow, I listen to the radio. A commercial comes on. I hear a mother's shriek, the sound of fire trucks. "Oh, God, please save my baby; she's in there. Please save my little girl."

More screams and shouts, then the fireman says, "Here's your little girl, ma'am."

The mother on the radio cries, "Thank you—oh, God, thank you." There's a sound of sirens, dogs barking, the little girl whimpering. Tears stream down my face as I drive home. Who am I weeping for? I wonder as I drive. Who needs saving?

Five years before, a man who had been a spy in Cambodia and then undergone some kind of conversion wanted to write a book about his experiences. He was a precept—as they call teaching assistants at the college where I taught—of a student of mine. The student asked if I would talk to the former spy about the book he wanted to write. Gabriel showed up at my office one afternoon. A short, stocky man, good-looking, strong and dark, he seemed like someone who could be a spy. He had a manuscript under his arm and asked if I would take a look at it.

I read the manuscript. It needed work; the story line had to be fleshed out. I didn't understand the narrator enough to understand his conversion: how he went from a military man to peace activist. Gabriel and I had several meetings about this. Then one afternoon he called to say that the university was contemplating a center for peace studies, and a planning committee meeting was being held that afternoon. Would I like to attend?

It was a warm spring day, and the sweet air smelled of magnolia as I walked briskly across campus, late as usual, to the small, dark building, with its many entrances, where the planning session was being held. An older man in a blue-jeans jacket was locking up his bike. "Excuse me," I said, "but I'm looking for a meeting of the Center for Peace Studies."

He spoke to me gently in a lilting voice that at first I mistook, as many people did, for a British accent. "I'm going there myself," he said. "I'll show you the way."

He opened doors for me, escorted me into a room where faculty members sat around on oversized couches. The discussion had already begun as we slipped inside. I gave the man a nod, then made my way toward the seat in the corner that Gabriel had saved for me.

Gabriel watched me coming in. In fact, he kept his eyes on me as I crossed the room. When I sat down, he asked if I knew the person I'd come in with. I told him I didn't; that I had just asked him how to get there. "Why?" I asked.

"Because that's the man who changed my life."

Later, after the meeting, Gabriel walked me to the train station, and Jeremy was standing on the platform. They talked, and I was introduced. Gabriel trembled slightly, and it was clear to me that he was a disciple in awe of this man who was responsible for his conversion from spy to peace activist. I noticed that the man was unshaven and his clothes looked somewhat dirty, his pants baggy. But he was tall and well-built, and he had a gentle, kind manner. His white-streaked black hair set off deep, dark eyes in a tanned face. You could see the strength in his arms, and his voice had that soft-spoken English accent that only later I would identify as an Upper East Side affectation. I estimated that he was twenty years older than I.

We spoke briefly on the platform until the New York–bound train came, then, since Jeremy and I were going the same way, we sat together on the train. We both had work to do, and for the first half hour or so we read. Somewhere around Metuchen, we began to chat. I don't remember what we talked about. Probably he asked me what I taught, what I did. I told him a few things. Then I asked about his work. He occupied an impressive chair at the university and had tremendous pressures in his life. He told me that his wife and boys lived in the city and that he had demands on him from everywhere all the time. He was supposed to go to San Francisco the next day, to Vancouver afterward, then he had a talk to give in Brussels. He didn't know how he could be in so many places at once. Everyone made demands on him.

"Why don't you just say no?" I asked, and he stared at me as if no one had ever made this suggestion before.

"Oh, it's not that easy," he said. "There are people who need me."

In Manhattan we said good-bye, went our separate ways. But then I encountered him on the platform of the subway heading uptown. "Going my way?" I asked with a laugh.

And he laughed as well. We were both going to Seventy-second Street. "Well, what are the chances?" He looked as if he were calculating them in his head. "They must be very small."

"It must be *beshert,*" I said, quoting my grandmother's favorite word, which roughly translates as "meant to be." He gazed at me uncertainly, and for the first time I saw that twinkle in his eye. "It's fate," I said.

Eight

The Reverend Schuller's gray robes complement his smooth gray hair, his soft gray eyes. He's big and he's jolly as a Labrador pup, with a welcoming smile that seems to take up most of his face and a strong, deep voice that fills the room. He raises his arms to welcome and bless us, saying how pleased he is to see the faces of so many children. It is Sunday, and the pews are filled with families in pastels.

His "Hour of Power" message is being broadcast live to its 1.3

million households. Looming above us in his pulpit, the Reverend Schuller—who is sixty years old and considered to be the Reformed Church of America's successor to Norman Vincent Peale—begins his sermon with a warning, but in an avuncular way. With Kate squirming in my lap, I listen as the reverend welcomes us. I feel somewhat taken in, charmed by his Cheshire cat grin, his silver hair.

But soon his warmth turns to worry, his brow furrows with concern. He is shaking his fist at us, scolding his children, who have gone astray. He warns us with stern words. The devil is everywhere, he says to his flock. You do not have to look far, he tells us. The devil is here. We glance around, look at one another as the reverend points. He is here and here, his fingers jabbing at the crowd. Evil can find its way to any heart. There are nods, amens, in this packed audience of relatively young, well-appointed, almost entirely white parishioners. Evil is all around us. Let us remember the measures we need to take, the steps we must follow in our mission.

Prepare to lead
Find a need
Clarify your creed
Expect to succeed
Do a good deed
Expect to believe
Prepare to bleed
No gain without pain
Resist your greed.

He's the Rod McKuen of the pulpit. Now his face grows stern, his eyes become fiery. He raises an admonishing finger.

The jungle is never far away, he tells his followers. The jungle is near. He points to his chest.

You don't have to go to deepest Africa or the center of Brazil. The heart of darkness is right where we are. Even in Orange County, the jungle is not far away. Even here in the City of God, the jungle is not far away. I want to help bring America back to civilization, to the man with the college degree and the fancy car and the big house. The jungle is never far from his heart.

Nine

Jeremy surprises us with a visit. He has to give a speech in Los Angeles and agrees to come down to Laguna for the weekend. When he calls from New York to tell me, I am thrilled, can't wait to see him. I offer to drive up to L.A. "Let me come and hear your speech," I beg, but he says it will make him too nervous.

His voice is warm, almost liquid, on the other end of the phone. It is like comfort food to me, smooth as vanilla custard. It was the words that first drew me in, that seduced me. And it is the words that keep me. I love to listen to the smooth way his mouth produces them. How they glide effortlessly from his lips. "I'll feel too self-conscious if I know you're there."

"But why? I've been there before."

"I just would."

Jeremy gives speeches all over the world. The rights of indigenous peoples, the illegality of nuclear weapons, the evils of intervention—these are topics he speaks on at length, off the top of his head. He is best speaking extemporaneously. Making it up as he goes along. I have seen him get up in front of five hundred people, with just a scribbled note card in his hand. Often he does not know what he's going to say until he's at the podium. I have heard him speak dozens of times, and it is always this same unfaltering manner.

Even now, as he explains why he doesn't want me to be there as he speaks, I feel as if he's making it up, thinking on his feet. I press him one more time. "I could meet you at your talk; then we could go out to dinner," but he says he'd rather see me afterward.

He has planned to drive down on Friday night after his speech, but when he arrives in L.A., he phones to say he'll come Saturday morning. He has a business dinner that evening. He did not anticipate this, but there are some people from India or New Zealand he must meet with. I am disappointed. Already our time is being whittled away. I know I should be used to this, but somehow I never am.

"Is it because you're having dinner with someone else?" I ask, meaning not a business associate.

"No, of course not," he says, his voice now whispery. I almost can't hear him.

Why does he need to whisper? I wonder if someone else is there with him in the room. I don't want to, but I think of Sigrid. There is no reason to think of her. He has assured me of this dozens of times, but still I do. Sigrid was a Danish woman who seemed to be around when I was pregnant. She'd call at odd hours, then suddenly show up in town. She was a minister with a guitar, and in low moments I referred to her as the singing nun.

Jeremy always told me that she was just a colleague, another peace activist like himself. But I became obsessed with her.

Though Jeremy has not mentioned her in months, I grow agitated just at the thought of her. I want to ask him now, but I don't dare. Is it Sigrid? But how could Sigrid be here?

When Jeremy arrives on Saturday morning, he sweeps us into his strong arms, places kisses on Kate's head. Yet I am held back, already feeling sour. Why couldn't he have come last night? Why couldn't I have gone there? If he'd taken the job in California, we'd be together. If we were married, I wouldn't be here. None of this makes much sense, and it seems as if my life is in fragments, pieces I can't pull together.

For breakfast I have prepared a buffet: bagels, lox, fresh fruit, a pot of coffee, fresh-squeezed orange juice. As we eat, he asks me how I am. He sits with Kate perched in his lap. "What do you want to do today?" I ask him.

"I just want to be with you," he says. I gaze at his gentle smile, hear his soft-spoken voice. I want to believe everything, and I do. After a leisurely breakfast outside on the patio, I offer to cut Jeremy's hair, which has grown long and unruly since we last saw each other. Jeremy has thick silver curls and a gray beard. He also has certain quirks. He won't eat oatmeal. He doesn't like my glasses resting on my head. He sits in the back of theaters. And he won't go into a barbershop. He won't let anyone, except the woman he's with, cut his beard. For a dozen years before me it was his wife. For the past five years it's been me.

I tease him as clumps of curly hair, soft as a baby's, tumble onto the patio, get scooped up by the wind. "So, Samson," I say, snipping at the air. "You're not afraid of Delilah?"

"I welcome her," he says with a laugh. I allow Jeremy his idiosyncrasies. He's had a strange life. His mother, who was some kind of tennis star, abandoned her children when Jeremy was seven and moved to Los Angeles. After the war she married a German, who never could explain to anyone's satisfaction where he had been during the war and who managed to get all her money turned over to him. Jeremy was raised by his devoted father and by a butler, who tried to slip into bed with him one night when he was twelve. Jeremy's sister used to run away, befriend people, then set their houses on fire. When I chide Jeremy about his quirks, his response is always the same. "I'm doing the best I can," he says, and in general I believe he is.

I trim his beard and his hair, and then we take Kate to the beach. On a whim, we drive down to the San Diego Zoo, where everything delights her. Jeremy takes her for a ride on a camel, and years later, when she is almost ten, she will say to me, "I rode on a camel when I was a baby, didn't I?"

She'll remember that Jeremy took her. She'll never call him her father, but she'll know that he took her for a camel ride.

That evening Jeremy and I go to Las Brisas for dinner along the cliffs. It is a fast-paced, trendy Laguna Mexican place, with a breathtaking view. Over drinks I say to Jeremy, "Why don't Kate and Ramona and I come and live with you next year? I can quit my job. I'll come home."

Jeremy thinks about this for a few moments. "That's a good idea," he replies with a smile. "I could use somebody like Ramona."

I am crestfallen. "That wasn't exactly the response I wanted," I tell him.

He pats my cheek. "Don't you know when I'm teasing you?"

"It doesn't feel like teasing," I reply.

I want to ask him for money. It is on the tip of my tongue, but I don't. Fifty dollars a week would buy me some weekend child care, a few things we need. Already Kate is outgrowing her baby clothes. I have not taken a penny from him (nor has he offered since she was born), but I'm having a hard time now making it on my own. Still, I think better of it. It's better to wait, to pace myself, until the time is right. When he realizes how much he needs us, that he can't do without us. Until then I'll be strong. I'll make do. Though I don't like taking it, though it makes me feel like a child again, the two hundred a week from my parents will get me through.

The next day we take Kate to the carousel on Balboa Island, where we go around and around, dozens of times. A balloon man who is about to call it quits for the day gives us all his balloons, dozens of them. We tie them to the stroller and run, laughing with her, up and down the boardwalk.

Ten

After Jeremy leaves, I move listlessly through my daily tasks, like some animal who has lost the will to live. Bathing, feeding myself, become efforts. I think it will work out with Jeremy if I can just be patient, but now I find I can't. Or won't. I decide to play that game of "let him come to you." At night as I try to put Kate down, I pretend I'm not waiting for the phone to ring. But of course I am.

I need friends, a group, something to belong to. In the late hours I find myself thinking about Reverend Schuller. How his smile makes you want to crawl into his lap. How I want to tell him everything that's on my mind. Maybe he'd listen. I'm thinking about this as I put Kate to bed and, as always, she screams. I try different things. Kate tends to sleep only eight hours—from about eleven to seven—with no naps. I have taken her to doctors for this problem. Her pediatrician in New York, Dr. Softness (this is his real name), said she needed more sleep. He told me to lock her in her room, just let her cry. It's what everyone does. I try to grade papers, listening to my daughter wail. An hour, two hours, go by. I can't stand it, so I tuck her in bed beside me, where she immediately drifts off to sleep.

One weekend night I put her in the car and drive up to the 405 and back until she is sound asleep. But as soon as I get home and take her out of her car seat, she is wide awake again. I am so tired, I think I will just drop. I carry her in, put her in her crib, and she starts to scream. "Stop it," I tell her. "Now go to sleep."

If someone else were here, I'd hand her to him. But there is no one. I close the door to her room and listen to her scream. Then I open the door. She's standing up in her crib, gripping the frame. Her face is beet red. She is so willful. "Now stop it! Go to sleep!" I am shouting at a ten-month-old child. I don't have these temper flare-ups often, but when I do, they frighten me. I grew up with shouting, with impulsive rages, and I know the damage they can do.

I pour myself a drink of brandy. Sip it at the kitchen table until I am calm. I wish I hadn't quit smoking. I go into the bathroom to splash water on my face. I can still hear Kate screaming as I gaze at myself in the mirror.

A decade ago, before I moved to Mexico, someone gave me a black eye. Even though it has been many years, the darkness returns when I am very tired. Like some phantom reminder of how low I can go, what I am capable of putting myself through. Now, gazing in the mirror, exhausted, I see it there—a patch of discolored skin, a half-moon rising beneath my eye.

I splash cold water on my face one more time, then go back

into the nursery. Kate hollers louder when she sees me. "It's all right," I tell her, scooping her into my arms. "It's all right."

In the end, Kate sleeps beside me. I know she should sleep in her own bed, but I'm too exhausted to fight it. I am so tired my arms ache. I have read books, articles, about the family bed. Primitive cultures always keep their kids with them. Otherwise they could be carried away by predators—coyotes, giant snakes, birds of prey. If a child sounds terrified, then perhaps she is.

Malachite: Helps clear out the energy of dark experiences that one cannot recall. Moonstone: Draws love. Rose quartz: Attracts love by teaching you to love yourself. While Angie works on my back, she instructs me in the properties of the stones. She drops them into my hand or places them on my body. "What do you feel?" she asks. "Do you feel warmth? Do you feel stronger?"

I don't feel a thing except their cold, hard surface. What I do feel is that my lower back hurts and now an old injury to my neck is acting up. "I don't feel anything," I tell her.

"Meditate," she tells me. "Listen to your body. What does it tell you about the stones?"

I try to meditate on what I do not feel, while Angie kneads my flesh. Only her hands make me feel better. The subtleties of the stones are lost on me. Five minutes after I leave her table and am driving home on the Pacific Coast Highway, the stiffness settles back into my bones.

In his poem "Looking West from Laguna Beach at Night," Charles Wright says: "It's nice to think that somewhere someone is having a good time,/And pleasant to picture them down there/Turned out, tipsy and flushed, in their white shorts and their turquoise shirts." From my patio I try to picture them as well, sipping margaritas, rings in their ears, sandals flopping on their feet. But thus far they elude me. Like me, Wright enjoyed the view from Laguna at night—the hill descending mercilessly to the shore, oil rigs visible off Long Beach, the smell of eucalyptus in the air. All of Western civilization seems to be at my back. And something else—Eastern, but with zinc oxide—something I have yet to understand lies ahead.

The Ring of Fire

Eleven

A geological map of the Pacific Rim reveals the Ring of Fire. This ring—the edge of the tectonic plates that form the floor of the Pacific Ocean—goes right through the center of Los Angeles. The circle of disaster, which extends from Alaska to Chile and across the sea to Japan and down through the South Pacific, brings with it earthquakes and volcanoes. The Ring of Fire is what makes islands appear or disappear, makes the Cascades blow their tops or Mount Pinatubo, dormant for six hundred years, suddenly explode.

The danger spews right out of the earth itself in the sweet-smelling tar that oozes from the La Brea tar pits. The tar pits, located in the heart of Los Angeles, served as a graveyard for the mammoths, sloths, wolves, deer, and saber-toothed tigers that roamed this region some 40,000 years ago. Horses and deer wandered into the tar pits to drink water and became entrapped. Wolves and tigers pounced on the captives and were themselves trapped. The tar sucked them all down, held them, and later gave back the bones.

But in this city, catastrophe lurks everywhere. From the ooze in the earth, the brush fires that sweep the canyons, the earthquakes, the mud slides that, gathering momentum, take million-dollar homes out in Malibu. In Joan Didion's novel *Play It as It Lays,* Maria Wyeth speeds aimlessly along the freeways while her car radio drones on with news of the latest flood, slide, quake, fire.

Perhaps more than any other place in Los Angeles, the La Brea tar pits show us what this city, wedged between the San Gabriel Mountains and the Pacific Ocean, is sitting on. What nature is capable of here. In the movie *Volcano,* the tar pits serve as the epicenter of disaster. Tar formed when pressure from the earth's plates squeezed oil to the surface. The first Spanish explorers, led by Don Gaspar de Portolá in the summer of 1769, were amazed to note, as they rode along what is now Wilshire Boulevard, "some large marshes of a certain substance like pitch . . . boiling and bubbling." The explorers wondered if this roiling bog wasn't the result of the half-dozen or so earthquakes they had felt since arriving in the region.

Sam Lauderstein, a friend of a friend from New York, has invited us for a late lunch on a Saturday afternoon. On our way to his place, Kate and I stop at the La Brea tar pits. We stand behind the chain-link fence that surrounds the bubbling watery muck, which emits the smell of hot asphalt. In the middle of the pit, a plastic bull mammoth trumpets for help. Its mate and baby trumpet back from the side. Kate and I sit on a bench in the park, observing the desperate scene in this pond. On the ground beside us, tar seeps from a newly forming pit.

Inside the museum, we peer at the haunting faces of animals in the agony of fighting their way out of the muck. The remains of a hundred lions have been found here; fifteen hundred wolves; a few intact mammoths; an awesome imperial mastodon. But human beings knew to stay away from the place that entrapped them. Only one human skeleton was ever found among the million fossils discovered in this pit—a woman, a murder victim whose skull was smashed nine thousand years ago. Then she was ceremoniously buried in the pits.

A hologram shows her skeleton, then how she would look if there were flesh on her bones. A native woman with haunting blue eyes and long black hair stares out at us, and I look back at her for a long time.

• • •

Sam Lauderstein lives in a white house on a residential street off Fourth Avenue, in the fringes between Venice and Santa Monica. I park, and Kate and I make our way to the porch and ring the buzzer. It takes him a while to come to the door, so long that Kate crawls up and down the wooden steps of his bungalow a few times.

Finally Sam arrives. He's wearing a black T-shirt, black slacks, black leather jacket, reflector shades. "Oh, shit, Mary, I can't believe I did this." He slaps his forehead. "I've been so busy. I forgot you were coming. I've got this meeting. You know, these German producers, they're only in town for a few days. . . . Did you drive up just to see me?"

"Oh, no," I tell him. "I've got lots to do."

"Really, God, I'm just so sorry."

He looks disheveled and distracted, as if he's on drugs. "This is so embarrassing. This meeting just came up. . . ." I can see he has dreams of making it big, of making something happen. I ask if we can use the bathroom, and reluctantly he invites me inside. The place is a mess. Clothes are strewn everywhere, dirty dishes sit on various surfaces, and everything reeks of beer. On the television is a handwritten note with the times of the major soap operas. I point to the sign. "What's your favorite?"

"Oh." He runs his hand through his hair. "I don't really watch them. I just plan to write for them. Twelve grand a week, you know."

"Oh."

"You just have to figure out the format, get the characters straight, that sort of thing. A friend's promised me a try-out."

I leave the poet, standing on his front porch. "Really," he says, "I'm sorry about this." He runs his fingers through his hair again. "We'll make another plan."

As I drive off, I see him standing there in his black jeans, black T-shirt, shades, as if he just walked out of a film noir.

On the way home, I hear that an accident on the 5 caused a seven-and-a-half-hour traffic jam. JC Penney is offering, in conjunction with the Orange County police, free fingerprinting "for kiddies who like to wander." Is Kate old enough to wander? Should I have her fingerprinted next Saturday? I decide not to head home right away. We drive over to Venice and walk the boardwalk.

We stroll past the souvlaki shops, the tie-dye stores. An aging hippie sells ankle bracelets she is making on the spot. A man carves a mermaid out of wet sand as people drop coins in his cup. On Muscle Beach, men with huge pectorals and bulging biceps are pumping iron inside a chain-link cage. Brown-skinned girls in bikinis body-sculpt their thighs, while roller skaters and joggers rush by. Their sharp exhalations sound like someone blowing on reeds. A tiny black man with stumps for legs and only one arm whizzes past us on a skateboard. Pausing just ahead, he does a little dance on his stumps, shaking his butt. Not far from him, a man with a sign that reads SINGLE FATHER: PLEASE HELP US sings with his daughter. She is perhaps five and has barrettes all through her hair. They put their faces together as she croons "I Shot the Sheriff." I hand Kate a dollar, which she lets fall into their hat.

Then I drive up the coast highway, and we stop at Malibu. A film crew is shooting on the beach; surfers ride the waves. I park along the side of the road and take Kate for a walk, her feet wading in the sea. We race up and down the shore, toss pebbles into the water. Suddenly there is a rustling among the waves. Something dark appears. I see a pair of dolphins not far from shore, so close I feel I could reach out and touch them. I pick Kate up, pointing. Dolphins, I say, hurrying with her into the surf. The water soaks my jeans. Kate throws her head back and laughs, as the dolphins frolic near us for what seems like a long time.

We lie in the sun to dry off, then stop for a burger. Kate devours french fries soaked in ketchup. We share an ice cream cone, then I find a supermarket, where I stock up on what we need. There's a sale on diapers, and I buy a box of forty-eight. It is dusk when we get on the 405, heading home. Kate likes the movement of the car, the wind on her face. Soon she is asleep, and she sleeps all the way home.

It is late when I get there, and Stan has parked in my space. I have discussed this with him before. I've asked him please to leave me a space to pull in behind the house. He's got his pickup, and his wife has her car, and he doesn't seem to see what the problem is. Now he's done it again, and I have to park down the block.

I have too many things to carry—groceries, the cooler, Kate. I take Kate up to the house first, slip her gently into her crib. Then I race back for the groceries. Before I even reach the car, I can hear her screaming.

Twelve

At night the eighteen-million-dollar Crystal Cathedral looks like a palace, beckoning, shimmering. Its amber glow illumines the otherwise stark and sterile site where it sits in the middle of the City, surrounded by its enormous parking lot. The night we go to attend the Christmas pageant, I feel like Cinderella arriving at the ball. Limos pull up, Mercedeses, all kinds of fancy cars.

As soon as I saw the ad, promising a cast of hundreds, special effects, live animals, and flying angels, I dialed (714) 54-GLORY. I thought Kate would enjoy the animals, and I wanted to see the angels. I ordered the best seats for the next available show, and ours are front and center.

Kate is mesmerized by the laser light show, the beams of yellow and red that crisscross above the hills of Bethlehem. The manger is replete with donkeys, goats, and lambs, and soon the Magi, bearing the usual frankincense and myrrh, arrive on camels. The Star of Bethlehem points like a ray at the cradle where a real baby lies. Kate's eyes widen as the camels cross the stage, but I grow bored, listening as the generic male voice recounts the story of Christmas. I expected twists, turns of phrase, a slightly better version than we're used to, but in fact it is the same old story, retold.

But suddenly there's a rustling. Around me, heads shoot skyward. I look up and there they are, floating above me. Angels with gossamer wings, pink-draped gowns, swish overhead in clouds of disco fog. A purple laser beam guides their ethereal flight. With feet discreetly crossed at the ankles, so you cannot peer up their skirts, the angels hurl and soar. They dip low, bodies outstretched, wings flapping, and the audience lets out a deep "Oh," then they rise high again, triumphant into the air.

Their chaste flight is made more convincing by their beatific smiles, and indeed I think to myself there is something angelic about them. I ignore the predictable epiphany of the Magi, the traditional songs, the too-often-told tale. Keeping my eyes aloft, I hear the swish of wings.

Thirteen

Carey McWilliams wrote, in his remarkable 1946 essay "Don't Shoot Los Angeles," that "While the folk-belief that new religious movements always arise in desert areas is certainly naive, nevertheless there is something about Los Angeles—its proximity to the desert, its geographical position (facing east and west), its history of rapid social change through migration—that leads me to believe some new religious movement is brewing here."

Emma Harding seconded his notion in her history of spiritualism. She said that cults thrive on the Pacific coast because of the wonderful transparency of the atmosphere, the heavy charges of mineral magnetism from the gold mines, and the passions of the forty-niners, which created "unusual magnetic emanations." I think of Reverend Schuller's creed about turning a mountain into a gold mine, and it all makes sense to me now.

McWilliams drew his findings from William York Tindall's *The Asian Legacy and American Life* (1945). In 1925 William Butler Yeats and his wife visited California. Mrs. Yeats, a medium, had a series of occult experiences in Los Angeles. For several nights her husband made notes on the occult communications she received. These notes became the basis for Yeats's remarkable volume *A Vision*.

While visiting Los Angeles, D. H. Lawrence met frequently with Lewis Spence, a Rosicrucian and an authority on the Atlantis legend. Much of the mysticism in *The Plumed Serpent* comes from his meeting with Spence. Later Aldous Huxley and his friend Gerald Heard, who were investigating telepathy, settled in Los Angeles. In *After Many a Summer Dies the Swan*, Aldous Huxley relates the attempt by Heard (Mr. Propter in the novel) to found a new cult in the region. Even Christopher Isherwood, arriving in Los Angeles as a brilliant young writer, soon fell under the influence of Heard's swami; he gave up literature and the movies, headed into the desert to meditate.

There is, Dr. Tindall notes, in all this "the strange recurrence of Los Angeles. To that city Heard, Huxley, and James M. Pryse, contriving to go East and West at once, retired to meditate, and it was there that Mrs. Yeats received the daemons. The attraction of this place for spiritual men and even for spirits is plain. But I am not sure I know what it means."

Hiking in the hills one afternoon, I meet my neighbors from across the way. I've seen them from time to time, two sisters who live in a bungalow not far from mine, and we stop and talk. They seem to know that I am new and I am renting the bungalow of the family that is away. I tell them that I am here from New York on a two-year teaching stint. They invite me and Kate for dinner the next night. I wear new khakis and put Kate in a sundress, bring a bottle of wine and a fruit salad. While they grill salmon and make rice pilaf, I think how nice it is to have someone cook for me. I tell them I can't see the seals on the rock from my house, and they lend me their binoculars.

Toward the end of the evening one of them mentions that she was working out in the gym the other day, and a black man was exercising next to her. "I've never smelled a black man before," she says to me. Then she asks, perhaps because I come from New York, "They smell different than us, don't they?"

"They smell the same to me," I say, making no attempt to hide my revulsion.

Kate gets drowsy, and I have the excuse to leave. I carry her across the road in my arms, the binoculars that I'll never return dangling around my neck. Instead of going inside, we sit on the patio. The moon is orange, just cresting the hills, and I put Kate on my lap. Pressing the binoculars to her eyes, I coax her to look. Then I put the binoculars to my eyes and gaze at the craters of the moon. They aren't very good binoculars. Everything seems so far away.

Fourteen

There was a time in graduate school when I contemplated doing a doctoral dissertation on the migratory patterns of Midwestern writers. Unlike Southern writers, who seem to stay put, the Midwestern writer tends to migrate. His or her work is filled with nostalgia for where he's been and perhaps a dose of exoticism for where he's gone. Fitzgerald, Hemingway, Dreiser, Twain, Cather, all wrote away, mainly from the East Coast or Paris. Twain once said that a writer becomes little more than a casual observer when he "steps from the state whose life is familiar to him." Yet he wrote his Mississippi masterpieces from Hartford. As a friend once said to me, "The Midwest is a good place to remember."

Unlike Northern California, whose writers—such as Steinbeck, Jack London, Robinson Jeffers, William Saroyan—were more or less indigenous, the writers of Southern California all came from somewhere else. The early writers about Los Angeles such as James M. Cain, Raymond Chandler, Nathanael West,

Aldous Huxley, F. Scott Fitzgerald, Dreiser, Isherwood, and, yes, even that Southerner Faulkner (who didn't stay long) were all migrants, coming in some cases reluctantly from somewhere else.

Dislocation and displacement is what Southern California has been about. Its workers have been migrant, whether in the fields or in the studio, and with their migrations they have brought with them the hodgepodge of their visions and beliefs. Southern California has largely been a place viewed by outsiders who are at once revolted by and drawn to its peculiarities.

I was eighteen when I left home, and every year for many years I was sure I would return. My parents often asked, though not too often, when I planned to move back. And I always said I would soon. When things were difficult for me, during some hard years, they assured me there would always be a place for me. But I never went. I went for visits. For a week or so at a time.

I went and stood by the shores of Lake Michigan, where I'd been a girl; I stood with my back pressed to the tree bent back in the wind along the bluff, at the place where so many years ago I'd planned my own death. This was also where I told myself my first stories. Half delusional myself, I was a pioneer girl defending her fort, a shipwrecked sailor, an orphan in flight. Or I was grown up and traveling in a strange land.

My tree is gone now, having eroded with the bluff, and long ago someone put up a fence, but I still drive thirty miles out of the city whenever I travel home, and I go to the end of the street where I grew up and gaze across Lake Michigan, which is where my life began.

When I think of Illinois, I am overwhelmed by certain sights and smells. My feet dragging through autumn leaves, ants crawling in the peonies, dead fish in the lake, the smell of fresh water, the crunch of the bodies of the seventeen-year locust. A line of girls walking to school in identical saddle shoes and camel-hair coats. The wind in my face as I bicycle home from school. Peanut-butter-and-marshmallow sandwiches sitting on a plate. My mother frying chicken, oil splattering on her hands. S'Mores and sweet, sticky fingers.

I come from the flat, even plains of the Midwest, where there is nowhere to hide. But I grew up along the shores of Lake Michigan, near the bluffs. I've always preferred fresh water, not salt. I had this flatness behind me but the lake ahead, and it was as if I grew up in two separate worlds. All the trails the Potawatomi made led to the lake, and many of those trails are the roads people drive on today. I have read that the shores of Lake Michigan have as much magnetism as the North Pole. I have always felt charged, drawn as if by some physical necessity back to the bluffs of the lake where I was born. Pulled back and repelled at the same time. And I know that this land has shaped me.

In 1967 and 1968 I lived in Paris. I lived on Rue Xaintrailles in the thirteenth arrondissement, in a large middle-income housing complex, with a woman named Joelle and her son, Jean-Michel. Joelle had lied on her application to have an American student live with her. She said that Jean-Michel was only fifteen, when in fact he was nineteen. I had just turned twenty and thought it might be nice to have a young French brother, but when I arrived at the apartment on Rue Xaintrailles I was greeted by a young man with silky blond hair, who was smoking a pipe. We had rabbit stew for dinner, and I was sick the entire night.

Jean-Michel was always home studying, as I was, and he spoke to me at all hours about Proust and politics and dreams. We walked through Paris on rainy days under an umbrella and ate in

Vietnamese restaurants and almost made love but never quite. We smoked our first cigarettes together and listened to melancholy Serge Reggiani songs as the sun set on the balcony of the apartment where we lived. Then Jean-Michel decided he couldn't date the girl living in the next bedroom, so he broke up with me, if you can break up with someone with whom you share a bathroom.

A few weeks later he brought home a girl named Valerie, who had brown hair and doelike eyes and seemed not very interesting to me. But Jean-Michel shut his bedroom door and played music with her on a long Sunday afternoon, while I smoked and listened to Piaf and stared at the gray Parisian sky. Afterward I began to wander. Trips to Italy to visit my roommate in Naples, London to see a friend. Then Jean-Michel went to America and I went to Jerusalem.

The story grows complex here. A lost address book, a handsome student who offers me lodging, a near rape, a night in the bus station. There is even a Greek Orthodox priest in this part of the story, who finds me weeping on my suitcase and leads me into the old Arab quarter, to a hotel called the Casanova. I can still see the beard of the priest, the long cross dangling from his neck. I left the Casanova to have breakfast and sat down and ordered an omelette. The young man across from me picked up his newspaper, and the headline read: MARTIN LUTHER KING ASSASSINATED: CIVIL WAR IN AMERICA.

I asked to read his newspaper, my hands shaking, and the man invited me to join him. He was a rabbinical student from Los Angeles, and we dropped acid on the road to Haifa and climbed into the hills where the prophet Elijah had preached. Then he followed me to Paris, where the May '68 revolution was taking place and the Sorbonne was flying the flag of anarchy and a two-story poster of Mao hung in its courtyard. We fled Paris, leaving on one of the last planes out of Le Bourget.

When I reached Illinois after being away a year, I brought this young man, Elliott, English for Elijah, the prophet of God. I lit up a cigarette in front of my father—something I'd never done in front of him before—and said I planned to marry Elliott and watched my father's face cave in. He still called me Pigeon then, a name he'd given me as a child because I was so restless, always fluttering around. Now anger cracked his face.

The young man flew to Los Angeles, and I followed him a week later, my father driving me to the airport, asking if this was what I really wanted to do. This was my first trip to California, and as I arrived in Los Angeles, Robert Kennedy's body was being transported down Olympic Boulevard. Then Elliott and I dropped acid in Disneyland. We took a ride that carried us into the crystal of a snowflake, and I saw myself surrounded by snow and then growing smaller and smaller, more compact, as we traveled that snowflake.

Afterward, on the Sabbath, I burned a cigarette hole in his mother's bedspread, and she wept not only over the hole in her bedspread but over our smoking on the Sabbath, and I was exhausted, so I flew back to Illinois. At dinner in a restaurant, my father asked me if I wanted a glass of wine or a screwdriver, and for some reason I started to weep. I wept in the restaurant bathroom and I wept in the car home and I got into bed and wept for two weeks.

When I stopped crying, my house was sold (this had been long planned by my mother) and we were getting ready to move into an apartment in the city, in a building my father's architectural firm had designed. On the day we were to move, I woke to the sound of my father trimming the hedges and mowing the lawn. The new apartment wasn't finished, and doorknobs kept falling off, locking us in empty rooms. My brother and a friend were arrested at the Democratic National Convention in Chicago for handing out bread, and the police broke their fingers.

I returned to college to help my roommate through an abortion. And my dog, who'd always lived in a house in the country, barked when he was left alone. The neighbors complained, so my mother gave the dog to the checkout girl at the A&P, and my childhood was gone.

Fifteen

My Fantasy Island student and I have a disagreement. He says I can't relate to what he's doing and it's my fault. I tell him I just don't understand his characters, who are mostly robots or fairy-like creatures who live in another world. Even robots need personalities, I tell him. I know he'll complain to my chairman and I'll be called back into the darkened office with the hovering owl.

That night, when I finally drift off, I have this dream: I am late, racing to class, and the chairman is standing at the door of my classroom. He informs me that my subject has been changed and I am now going to teach Martian literature. Martian literature? I ask him. You mean like H. G. Wells, Ray Bradbury? I suppose I could do this, I tell myself, but he says, "No, indigenous Martian literature." Indigenous? What am I going to say? I haven't read the work.

Trembling, I walk into class and find eight hundred students, all green, with antennas. I begin speaking about what it's like to live on the fringe of the universe, to be marginalized in the solar system, when suddenly eight hundred hands go up. A horrendous buzzing begins. It seems that Martians all have to go to the bathroom at the same time, and now they rise, stomping out, stampeding over me.

At night when Kate won't sleep and I rock her endlessly, I think about the angels. I see their wings flapping, their legs neatly crossed. What would make a grown woman do such a thing? A deluded self or an act of faith? I used to believe in things—that God would stop my airplane from crashing, that God would make something come my way. I made pacts from time to time. If I give up this, will you give me that? If I pass this test, won't I win some prize? Destiny, karma, fate. Like my grandmother before me, I've spit in the air to keep evil away.

I thought that if I lived a certain kind of life, good would come. Now I'm not so sure. Things seem beyond my control. I'd give anything to believe again. Somehow I have lost the way. I ponder this as I head into the kitchen for a glass of brandy, leaving Kate screaming in her crib. I drink one, then two glasses, and in the morning my head aches.

When I can't listen to Kate cry anymore, I scoop her up, lay her in bed beside me. Sipping the brandy, I watch her settle into her child's sleep. Dreams of milk and breasts or of fluffy things. But I cannot rest. The wind chimes keep me awake. The bronchial cough has deepened, and there are animal noises. I read in a local newspaper that fifty-six mountain lions roam in the hills above my house.

On weekends I can't get anything done. Unless I wake up at five (which I sometimes do), I can't even take a shower, let alone prepare for my classes. If I had fifty dollars extra a week, I could get a little more help. A student, maybe, to spell me while I grade papers, read, maybe even take a nap. I think about it for a while.

Then I call Jeremy, and we talk about this and that. He asks how I am doing, and I tell him that frankly, money is becoming a problem. I know this is the last conversation Jeremy wants to have. "It's hard for me to get anything done on the weekends," I say. I don't ask directly for what I need, but he can't miss the point. Still, it hurts my pride to ask.

"I wish I could help out," he says. He hems and haws. "I have so many burdens, so many expenses."

"I understand," I tell him, "but I'm trapped. I can't go anywhere. I can't get anything done."

The boys need things, he tells me. Stereos, special schools, clothes. He just doesn't have the cash. Ask your parents, he says. I don't tell him that they're already giving me what they can.

I don't want to talk about money. I miss him. That's the most important thing. He misses me too, he says. We chat for hours about our work, our friends, current events, local gossip, whatever pops into our heads. And then we hang up the phone, and he's gone.

One Sunday afternoon I call an acquaintance from the university to see if he wants to go to the beach. When I reach him, he says he has to hang a venetian blind. He says he'll call me later, but he never does.

Angels

Sixteen

The angels sit in a circle, beaming at me. They don't have halos, but they may as well. Their goodness is disconcerting. The peaches-and-cream skin, the twinkling eyes, the wide grins. I cannot bear so much joy, though each assures me she has paid her dues. They seem somewhat interchangeable, though, in their white shirts and dark pants, as they go around, introducing themselves. There's Sandra, Kerry, Monique, Betsy, Alisha, and Glynna. They are all in their late thirties or early forties, trim and fit, due to their angel regime, and ready to share their stories with me.

It has taken several weeks to get this interview. Posing as a reporter for a major East Coast newspaper, I phoned the Crystal Cathedral public relations office and said that I am doing a Christmas special on their angels. I'd like to interview the women who fly. I was told that the angels were out of town, but they would be back soon.

Now we sit at a circular conference table, and the six angels smile at me. As I scribble on my steno pad, their spokesperson tells me how they attend "flight school," where they go through weeks of rigorous training and rehearsals. There are special ways for projecting themselves—the movement of the hands, the arch of the back. They cannot weigh more than one hundred twenty pounds, and many have been on stringent diets to maintain their weight. Their aerial displays are carefully choreographed for safety and appeal. Only once did something go wrong with a wire, and an angel from San Jose crashed into the manger, knocking a camel, two magi, and the baby Jesus himself out of the way.

Glynna, who seems the most open, tells me her story. "I weighed a hundred and sixty pounds," she tells me, the smile never leaving her lips. "My husband had just left me, my children were grown. I had nothing in my life that mattered to me. I was alone, just struggling to get by." A dark shadow passes over her eyes, a rim of sadness is there. "Then a friend got tickets to the Easter pageant, and it changed my life." Glynna came to the director of the Christmas pageant and said she wanted to fly. "So lose forty pounds and quit smoking, and we'll make you an angel-in-training." Now Glynna has flown in several pageants and helps train apprentice angels.

Each angel has her tale to tell—divorce, betrayal, loss. Not so different from mine, I think. Betsy overcame illness and her husband's abandonment. Kerry had suffered the death of a child. Each found her purpose in flight. We spend an hour or more, swapping stories. "And what about you, Mary?" one of them asks. I tell them I am a single parent, raising my child alone, at least for the time being. They nod their heads. Nothing is new to them. They've heard it all.

As we say good-bye, they want to know when my article will appear. "Around Christmas," I tell them with a twinge of guilt, not sure if any story I'll write about them will ever be published. I've lied to angels. What am I doing here? What has brought me to this place?

After the interview, the head of public relations informs me that they ask all reporters who interview the angels to fly. "I'm sorry," I tell her. "I don't understand."

"We'd like you to fly," she says. Perhaps she suspects that I am disingenuous. The angels sitting across the table are smiling, bemused, but now their faces look distorted.

"But I don't weigh a hundred and twenty pounds at the moment."

"It's all right for a short flight," she tells me.

On a high platform at one end of the church, Peter Foy's riggers are waiting for me. They have big grins on their faces as they strap something over my shoulders, pull a cord through my crotch. The wire fits snugly at my waist, not on my back, where it seems natural it should be. Below me, distances seem vast. Diminutive people in small tour groups begin to look my way. "Try to keep your shoulders back. Stay upright," one of the riggers advises me.

"What happens if I don't?" I ask. He just shrugs. Already I feel the wire tugging at my waist. I am being lifted high into the air, then swung out into the empty space, careening through the apse of the church. The light streaming in from ten thousand windows illumines my path as the wire takes me higher and higher, then flings me forward. Below, the tour groups pause. Faces look up at this miracle of flight as a reluctant angel, screaming, fighting, begging to be released, passes above their heads.

Some shield their eyes to watch my transit. Others begin to laugh. I can see the smiles crack on their faces, hands covering mouths. They know that I am no beatific creature but an ambivalent one, pleading to be set free. In midair above the altar there is no turning back. The wire carries me farther, yet I feel myself descending, falling forward. Wishing the wire were at my back, not around my waist, I start to plunge, to belly flop, to go down flat.

Behind me, below me, laughter resounds. A tour group from Iowa—blue-rinse women in lime-green leisure suits, little name tags gracing their chests—cracks up. Old women laugh, men in pastels point at me. The spectacle is not lost on them. This is what I get for the sin of pride, for flying too close to the sun. Any moment now I'll tumble head over heels, spinning in hopeless circles around my wire.

As I am flung farther into the center of the cathedral, I begin to try and right myself. I kick my legs, but this only sends me more out of control, spinning like a top. The wire around my waist is barely enough to support me, or so it feels. Now, tentatively, I move my arms, and this seems to correct my balance. Slowly at first, I move my hands up and down, until the motion helps me straighten out, get my bearings. Then it seems to hold me aloft. I raise my arms again, this time beating the air faster and faster. The more swiftly I beat my arms, the steadier I become. Through my screams and the laughter I hear below me, I wave my arms faster and harder, until it becomes clear in midflight that if I don't flap, I'll flip.

I forget about the wire. Now it is my arms that sustain me. I flap harder, head erect, chest forward, my arms waving in ever-larger, more expansive swirls. I swim in air, a condor, an eagle, my hands graceful now, poised. I begin to soar, up and down, a bird, entrapped in the cathedral as I have seen birds flutter in the dome of Nôtre Dame, Saint Patrick's. But there is freedom in this flight. My wings beat, my heart pounds as I glide back and forth above the nave, now it seems without wire but screaming still, eighty feet in the air.

I soar and dive, catch the wind, my wings flapping, hands flowing. I dip and climb, hurtling through the cathedral, oblivious now to the tour groups, who have ceased their laughter below, as close as I've ever come to God.

Seventeen

The next day I can't get out of bed. My spine aches as I turn. After several attempts, I twist my whole body to the left until my feet touch the floor. Pain shoots through me as I realize I have thrown my back out. This doesn't feel like a job for Angie. In the spiral notebook my landlady prepared for me, giving all the practical details of the house and the town, she listed a local chiropractor. I make my way into my car, easing my legs in, and drive down the hill to his office.

His waiting room is crowded, which I take to be a good sign. On the table there are the usual magazines—*People, Vogue, California Life, Doggy World.* I flip through *Orange County Life.* Then a copy of the plum-colored "Edenic Light Center Newsletter" catches my eye, and I begin to leaf through it.

The center, which is only a few miles from my house, offers seminars in crystal healing, which Angie has already started me in, past-life regression, a daylong workshop in healing your inner child, another in transformation. It also mentions that the next night Wanda Joy, who is an extraterrestrial walk-in—whatever that is—will channel Ashtar.

I hear my name called and see the young, smiling doctor waiting for me. He pokes at my spine, checks me over. Then he asks me what I've been doing to throw out my back in this way. "I've been flying as an angel," I tell him.

He doesn't skip a beat. "Well, next time," he says, "do some stretches first."

• • •

It is literally a dark and windy night as I drive along the Pacific Coast Highway. Why I have decided to go to the Light Center that night is somewhat of a mystery to me. I am not completely unschooled, however, or even particularly a disbeliever, in the world of the occult, the unusual, the alternative side of life.

I paid part of my way through graduate school working as a Gypsy. I wore a purple turban and a peasant blouse, lots of bracelets, and was hired for parties, where I read palms and tarot cards. I had been taught how to read palms by an Indian mystic who was a friend. Before he disappeared somewhere in the Punjab and became a saint, he said I had "the gift."

I wasn't particularly good with the cards, but my friend was right; I seemed to have a knack for reading palms. I wasn't sure how I did this, and at times it frightened me. I could look into jagged lines on trembling hands and see long illness or health, a child's birth or death, untapped talents, failure or success. Once, I looked at a girl's hands and saw no future, and indeed this girl had no future.

At a party near Columbia where I was being well paid to tell fortunes, a woman held out her hands and I shook my head. "What is it?" she asked. "What do you see?" I told her I was tired, that I could do no more, but she insisted. We went into a bedroom, and I told her I saw suicide there. She wept. Her husband had just left her, and night after night she stood beside the subway tracks. "Get help," I told her. I believe I saved her life. I stopped taking money for readings after that.

I cannot explain how I see what I see. Somehow the hands reflect the soul. It is an odd, mysterious talent even to me—one I use sparingly.

As I make my way to the Edenic Light Center, I wonder what

others will see. If perhaps someone can tell me what is in store. What this time in my life is all about. What awaits me on the other side.

The light center is upstairs in a little mall, and mine is one of the only cars in the lot. The Santa Ana blows, and clouds brush across the face of the moon. It is an eerie night as I climb the wooden steps to the door that reads: EDENIC LIGHT CENTER. At a small card table in a room of fluorescent lights, three teachers greet me. They introduce themselves as an aura healer named Sky Radiance, who hands me her business card ("Dial RAD-IANCE"); a past-life regressionist; and Wanda Joy, the channeler of Ashtar. The winds have kept others away, and that night I am their only student.

The idea comes to them that they can work on my aura, help cure me of a few ills, and see what it is in my life that is the source of this lingering sadness. What is keeping me down, holding me back. The three women have me lie down on the floor while they close their eyes, check my energy fields by running their hands over my aura, read my palms, meditate on my past, ask for help from their various ethereal sources. After a while they declare that I have not yet given birth to my daughter.

So I ask, "Who is the baby-sitter watching back home?"

They explain that though I have literally given birth, I have not yet released my daughter into the world. It is true that there were difficulties surrounding Kate's birth. Jeremy, who had refused to attend Lamaze classes, showed up when I phoned him from the hospital. So did my friend and birth coach, Michael. The nurses were confused because I had two men in the labor room. I had difficulty breathing in sync.

Finally Rochelle, my main nurse, asked the two men, as well as my friend Nancy, who had come to photograph the event, to wait outside. Rochelle turned to me and said, "I don't know what you have going on here, but you'd better decide who you want with you in the delivery room." In the end, no such decision would be necessary. After twenty-two hours of labor, the doctor said he was doing a caesarean, and I told him I didn't care if he did a lobotomy.

When I mention the caesarean to my instructors at the light center, their faces beam with sudden recognition. They explain that caesarean birth is not real birth—which they will facilitate by helping me reenact my labor. They ask me to lie on the floor and assume the position I was in while laboring. As I stretch out, legs raised, they run their hands over my body. I can feel their warmth.

Wanda Joy invokes the assistance of her extraterrestrial fleet. The past-life regressionist declares that I died giving birth in a previous life; and Sky Radiance tells me she can see the holes where my aura has collapsed, like the ozone layer. I lie there feigning labor while they midwife me.

They tell me to breathe, pant, push, push harder. "You can do it, Mary," one of them says. Sky Radiance promises I won't die. The regressionist assures me I'll be well. Wanda says all the universe is on my side. I feel their hands upon me, urging me on. Around me they pant and push and breathe, and I join them until at last, the four of us exhausted, they declare me reborn.

Eighteen

At the end of *The Day of the Locust,* Tod watches the gathering ferocious crowd and muses, "Where else should they go but California, the land of sunshine and oranges. Once there they discover that sunshine isn't enough. They get tired of the oranges, even avocado pears and passion fruit. Nothing happens. They don't know what to do with their time." Nathanael West, who died in obscurity in a car crash on the Pacific Coast Highway, knew something about California and its broken dreams. He understood that people came here to reinvent themselves, but they also came to die.

Where *The Day of the Locust* ends, *They Shoot Horses, Don't They?* begins. It is not for nothing that Horace McCoy's dance marathon in that novel takes place at the end of the Santa Monica pier and that Gloria cynically echoes Scarlett O'Hara's "After all, tomorrow is another day." Gloria says, "The big break is always coming tomorrow," but for Gloria and Robert, two random human beings thrown together at a bus stop, there are only tomorrows where something is supposed to happen that doesn't. This novel also ends in death "out there in that black night on the edge of the Pacific."

But I came here, or so I thought, to live. Yet I cannot find my way. I live in a place where the days are too light and the nights too black, where the walks lead nowhere and I have to turn back. My mind is full of jingles I hear on the radio. I hum Beach Boys tunes wherever I go. "I wish they all could be California girls . . ."

In the morning Kate eats the carpet. She eats paper and books. She literally devours them. On the beach she eats handfuls of sand. I try to stop this, but if I look away, she does it again. I call the doctor, and he says he doesn't know why babies do such things, but it doesn't seem to kill them. I read somewhere that they get minerals, like the salt (she sneaks handfuls of salt at home when she thinks I'm not looking). Still, strangers tap me on the shoulder. Your baby is eating sand.

In an interview, Isabel Allende said that as an exile, "You never feel that you can plant any roots anyplace else. It takes a very long time to understand that your roots are within yourself." I seem to have lost the sense of what those roots may be. I long for other places where I've been, places I've called home. I seem to have lost the way, the thread.

Yet exile has its rewards. Somehow I manage to pull myself together, get some things done. I wake up early, well before dawn, and ease my way out of bed, where Kate has usually spent the night. If she awakens, the time to prepare my lessons is gone; if she sleeps late, perhaps I can even get some writing done. For weeks I wasn't writing, but I've begun again. I've taken the novel I was working on out of the drawer and put it on top of the desk. This must be progress, I tell myself. I begin to leaf through its pages, but it is as if some stranger I've been corresponding with has asked me to read her work. Still, I sharpen my pencils, I begin to scribble in the margins again, thinking of what a friend once said: The only way out is to write your way out.

I know this is true. Years ago, I had a dream in which I was walking down a street in Paris and came to a café. The name of the café was Leave All Hope Behind, Ye Who Enter Here. Strange name for a café, I thought. But inside I saw Gertrude Stein, Fitzgerald, and Hemingway, sipping Campari and soda. I sat at a little round table, and as the waiter took my order, "Campari and soda," my table sank into a deep, dark hole, farther and farther into the earth.

I was in an oubliette, one of those places where they dropped prisoners during the Middle Ages and forgot about them. Staring up, I knew there was no way out, that it was dark as far as the eye could see. Suddenly six pallbearers arrived, bearing a coffin, then they disappeared. I understood that it was my destiny to open this coffin, that the way out lay inside. Gently I raised the coffin lid, and it turned into a rolltop desk and paper for eternity.

A memory comes to me as I sit in my little office, staring up at the Irvine hills. It is a rainy March, dreary, decades ago, and I am four or five years old. My father sits at a card table, papers spread out. He is paying bills, doing his taxes, whatever it is grown-ups do. On the table are legal pads, long yellow ones, and he writes furiously with a big black pen. I am bothering him. I know this. I must be, because he writes something across the top of a yellow legal pad. "Here," he says, "this is your name. It says 'Mary.' Now copy it."

I want to please him. I always want to please my father, which isn't easy to do. He is an exacting man, and I feel a very large burden with the task he has set out for me. This is the first time I remember having pencil and paper in my hand. There must have been crayons and drawings before, but what I remember is that pencil and pad. I can still see the pad perfectly, those long yellow sheets, the thin green lines. I still write on such pads; they are all over my house. I scribble on them night and day.

At the top of the pad my father has handed me is a word, the first word I remember seeing written down. My name. I begin.

Gripping the pencil in my hand, I copy what I see. It is cold in the room, a draft comes in, but it is warmer on the floor, though the gray rug is scratchy. I want to stop, ask my father to help me. I want to know if I am doing it right, but his head is down, his eyes on the work he is doing.

It is a mystery to me, but I begin. I work the letters slowly, one at a time. I work them again and again. If I make a mistake, I stop and begin once more. I do this until I am satisfied. Until I see that I have written what my father has written at the top of the page.

MARY, it says. MARY. I take the pad to him. He does not look up as I slip my pad onto the table where his papers lie. My nose comes just to the edge. I am standing on tiptoes, peering at the tabletop. I see his finger come down. "The *R* is backward," my father says. I look at his finger, study the *R*. Even now I can see his finger, pointing on the page.

He gives the pad back to me, and I sit on the floor and begin again.

I'm flat broke. I've gone over everything, every penny, and I seem incapable of making ends meet. Between the rent, the food, the car payments, miscellaneous household expenses, I can just make it to the end of the month. After that I'm squeezing blood out of a stone. And I'm going deep into credit card debt. When money from writing trickles in, I use it to pay off the debt or buy Kate new clothes. I could ask Mom for more, but it doesn't seem right. Jeremy seems like the good choice, but after our last conversation I resist. When he calls that night, he says he'll be here at Christmastime for sure. Plan something nice, he tells me.

When he's here at Christmas—I'll ask him then. Fifty dollars a week. Two hundred a month. Surely he wouldn't deny me that.

I miss you, I tell him. In my mind I am sure that this is just a stage. He is afraid of commitment. He has been burned several times. I know we can make it work. Every night, I wait for his call and we speak for an hour, two hours, Kate resting in my arms.

I always laugh at his jokes, and he laughs at mine. This is just a phase. Yet I find I cannot sleep. I am up late at night, listening to the bronchial cough, to wind chimes. I stay up, sifting through papers, cleaning my room.

One night I go through all the bills, trying not to panic at those I cannot pay. The phone bill is definitely too high and will have to wait. So will American Express, which I decide not to use anymore. Looking for a new checkbook, I find, lying at the bottom of a drawer, Wanda Joy's business card. It has a rainbow, arching through heart-shaped clouds. Small hearts flutter around the rainbow in this sky. I give it a long stare—the sweeping letters of her name, the bold "Channeling for Personal and Spiritual Fulfillment."

I keep the card in my pocket, walk around with it for a few days. Perhaps Wanda will have some answer for me.

One afternoon, sitting in my office at school, waiting for a student, I find the card again, in the pocket of my jeans. I finger it, flatten out the rainbow, then give her a call. Wanda answers and seems to remember me right away; she almost seems to have anticipated my call. "Oh, yes," she says. "I thought I'd hear from you."

I want to ask her how she knew, but I am wary of the answer. We start to chat, and I ask her to tell me exactly what she does. How does she make contact with Ashtar?

Wanda explains that she does no out-of-body trances. That what she does are called light trances. She prefers to skip the astral and planetary planes and go straight to the source of light, moving immediately into the intergalactic spheres. In this way she is able to make herself available to the extraterrestrials who are circling the earth. She tells me she is a "walk-in." Like my beauty shop? I ask her, and reluctantly she agrees. Wanda explains that she has reached a high level of consciousness, and extraterrestrials who orbit the earth are able to use her as a medium to communicate their messages to earthlings.

There is a knock at my door. The late student has arrived, with stories of traffic jams, various delays. "Just a moment," I shout at my door. "Extraterrestrials communicate through you?" I say, feeling the need to repeat what Wanda just said.

"That's right." As she talks, I'm aware of her accent for the first time. Slightly British, with a twang that I later assume, correctly, to be Australian. Casually I ask her how long she's been here.

"What do you mean by 'here'?" she asks. "Do you mean earth?"

Nineteen

Everything in California comes from somewhere else. The plants, the animals, the people, even the snails. The eucalyptus and the acacia come from Australia; the pepper tree is from South America. The eucalyptus still blooms during Australia's spring. The rat, the mouse, the English sparrow, the pheasant, are all imports. Even the weeds, the water, and the soil have been brought here from somewhere else.

Only the climate is indigenous to this place, and it is the climate that accounts for everything else: the hot, dry weather at the edge of a roiling sea. Before, there were tar pits and scrub desert. Now there is golf and tennis and mansions perched just this side of disaster. Mud, fire, earthquake, are what is here, along with that weather.

Miraculous curative powers, attributed to the weather, brought invalids and health seekers and, in their wake, a variety of psychics, healers, spiritualists, utopians. "Migration," Carey McWilliams writes in "Don't Shoot Los Angeles," "is the basic explanation for the growth of cults in Southern California."

And certainly over the past century or so they came. The movements had names such as The Mighty I Am, Krotona, Mankind United, Ham and Eggs, and later Heaven's Gate. They came here and flourished under charismatic leaders such as Katherine Tingley (the "Purple Mother" who founded the Point Loma Theosophy Movement) and Aimee Semple McPherson (of the Foursquare Gospel), who apparently drowned, then miraculously, to the delight of her followers, reappeared. There was Edgar Holloway, who claimed to have arrived upon Mount Shasta on a flying fish.

The Idea of the West is nothing new. It was carried from Europe across the Atlantic, and then across the whole continent. The movement went by many names—Manifest Destiny, California Dreaming—but it boiled down to a belief that natural right had precedence over birth rights, that man must rule his environment, impose his will upon nature and the land and transform it into wealth. Los Angeles, fashioned out of the desert, made possible by water diverted from Owens Valley, is perhaps more than any other American city one that invented itself.

In the pursuit of happiness, the search for El Dorado,

somehow the seekers made their way here. For his "democracy project," the monologuist Spalding Gray studied the triangle of American power centers—New York, Los Angeles, and Washington. In Los Angeles he attended a battery-charging meeting where people dressed like Roman cardinals and for two hours received energy from a flying saucer. Gray said in an interview, "What terrifies me about Los Angeles is that I haven't found anyone who admits to any doubt."

The gate clangs, and Wanda Joy walks up my brick path, wearing a pink jumpsuit. Her trim scarlet hair is cut short, punky, and she wears flying-saucer earrings. When I open the door, she extends her hand, the nails flashing purple iridescence. Assorted crystals dangle from around her neck.

I show her the way in, offer her something to drink. Wanda shakes her head. She is all business as she settles into the couch. I have invited her for a private session, to see if she can channel Ashtar in my living room. I have told her on the phone that this is a time of change for me, of difficult transition and flux. She assures me that Ashtar knows about change and flux, and he can guide me on the right path.

Wanda informs me that she will channel some of the spirits and deities with whom she is in contact. She mentions Lenduce, who is an ascended being, Archangel Lord Michael, Isis, Helios, and Saint Germaine. Wanda is able to make herself available to the highest level of consciousness, where she is contacted by the spirits. She is merely the vessel; they send their messages through her. Ashtar, she explains, is the intergalactic commando, and through him all extraterrestrials come to her.

I nod, trying to take this in. It is a bit more than I bargained for, but I'm game. She explains that in a few moments Ashtar will speak through her. Briefly we chat like friends. She asks about my life, what's been going on. I blurt it all out. The baby, the new job, the unrequited love, my financial woes. "I'm not sure how I'm going to make it," I say.

She assures me that soon the deities and spirits to whom she will make herself available will have a comforting message for me. I want to believe that there will be a message that will make sense, that will tell me what to do. That I will find comfort in what Ashtar has to say. Then she asks me to close my eyes, and she goes into her trance. I do not close my eyes. Instead I stare at her. The flying-saucer earrings, the scarlet hair.

Suddenly Wanda begins to talk, but it is not Wanda. It is someone I don't know. A weird high, squeaky voice says, "We greet you, my friend, we who are speaking to you from the highest plane of consciousness, we who are members of the intergalactic fleet of starships circling the earth. We greet you and welcome you and embrace you into our fold. I am Ashtar, commander from the ethereal plane. You have seen our lights flickering in the night, passing among the stars. You have wondered at our comings and goings. Now we are here to respond to your questions, to offer the answers you seek as to why you inhabit the planet you call earth."

I can't help myself. I begin to laugh. I am glad Wanda has her eyes closed. I clasp my hand over my mouth and listen as Ashtar continues.

"We are here to inform you of our mission and to help prepare your way to the next level. We are involved in a higher purpose, and you are part of that purpose. You are the seeker for truth, but still you do not understand why you are here or where you are going. You have not begun to realize your great potential because you do not yet know your purpose. Now we have come to show you the path.

"We will build a Golden Circle of souls to create our earth-based unit. With the brothers and sisters of Other Worlds we will mobilize our strength. We are a family. We have made contact so that at last you will end your aloneness. So that at last you will understand the mystery of your planetary existence."

I am not sure what to do. As Ashtar rambles, I find myself growing weary, feeling a bit alone. I wish Ashtar could understand what I am feeling. Just then Wanda grows tense; her brow furrows. Something seems to displease her. "You see, my friend, your head is filled with shoulds and should-nots. You are listening to everyone but yourself. We are here today to tell you to listen to yourself. You are worthwhile, what you think is worthwhile. But you do not know how to listen.

"We light beings who circle the earth, we greet you and welcome you as one of our workers. You have the power within yourself to heal. You have the power to move to the next level of consciousness. You are too earth-bound, you are living on the ground. Ascend, rise, you must ascend. You do not know how free you are. You do not know what you are capable of. You have not begun to tap into your potential. This is the time of your transformation. Ascend. Only then will your soul be free."

One day just after I graduated from college, my father phoned to inform me that my brother had been dipped in a river in Oklahoma. I was heading out the door to attend a Buddhist ceremony in Cambridge and told my father I'd call him back. I was given my mantra that day and have held on to it ever since, the only secret that, for some reason, I've never told. To this day, on an airplane or in my office at school, on a subway car stopped midtunnel, I can recite it, and twenty minutes later I blink back into the world.

My brother, a born-again for a while, was concerned that we'd all go to hell if we didn't embrace Jesus. He sent us lists with proof that the Second Coming was at hand. He got very upset that we were still Jews (though I told him I'd embraced the Buddhist faith), because he wanted to see us in heaven, where he was going. He'd call late at night and beg me to accept Jesus Christ as my Lord. Fortunately this phase didn't last long. As for me, I was an Orthodox Jew for only a millisecond, but I have been lost at times and struggled to find the way.

My grandmother never kept kosher until her husband died. It was guilt, my mother said. Superstition was more my peasant grandmother's thing. She'd turn a compliment into an insult, to keep the kine-ahura away. Spit into the sky. My mother said it's all nonsense. For her there's no karma, no afterlife. What you see is what you get.

There's something about what Wanda says that seems vaguely familiar. I don't think it's coming from a starship, but it's coming from somewhere. I'm just looking for peace, I tell myself after Wanda leaves. And answers. Whichever comes first.

Freeways

Twenty

The morning after Wanda's visit, I wake to a perfect day, as they all seem to be here. A golden-blue sky shimmers overhead, cloudless, burning. Kate plays on the floor as I read the newspaper, sipping coffee. I hear Ramona clattering in the kitchen. An oddly peaceful feeling comes over me. Kate has taken a book, *I Am a Little Lion,* off the shelf and turns the pages slowly. I watch her turning pages, playing with her toys.

Stepping outside, I watch a sheet of rain on the ocean, miles away. Sea lions bark from the rocks offshore, but I cannot see them from where I stand. Ramona looks at me sadly from the kitchen, and when I ask what is wrong, she says she misses her son. She tries not to miss him, but when she sees me with Kate, she can't help it. She has tried not to mention him too much, but it is becoming more and more difficult to be away from him.

Kate scoops up snails from the garden, sticks her thumbs into their green slime. Of course Ramona wants her son with her. I can't imagine being without Kate.

"What do you plan to do?" I ask her.

"I was hoping I could go and get him, then bring him to live with us here."

Already the house feels small. I'm not sure where a six-year-old boy would sleep, but Ramona has thought this through. "I could have the living room; he could be in the room with Kate. They would be playmates."

Somehow I feel the weight of the responsibility I have taken on. Another child. Another woman's son.

"Why don't you go get him at Christmas," I tell her.

She smiles, tugging her hair over the place on her head where it doesn't grow.

Because I have a baby who will not sleep and an automobile, two things I've never had before, I begin to drive. I put Kate in her car seat and drive up to Los Angeles. We go to Watts Tower, to the Getty Museum. Bill, a friend of a friend, has a bungalow in Venice, tucked in a grove of banana trees.

Bill gives me a bear hug, lifting me off the ground. When he does, all my vertebrae crackle. He is very kind to us. He drives a red Thunderbird convertible, which will be totaled a few years later when a guy runs a light and slams into Bill on the driver's side (he'll survive but be in the hospital with head injuries for weeks). He wants to make it in the celluloid world, like just about everyone else I've met around here, but he's also willing to make me mint tea, to let Kate pluck leaves from his banana tree.

We like this spot on a side street in Venice. It is cool in the shade, and we can sit in the yard for hours, doing nothing. When I take a nap, Bill walks Kate down the street to visit some dogs. Later, when he takes us out for Thai food, he asks me about my life and holds Kate so I can eat. I think I should forget about Jeremy, but I can't. It might be nice to be with a man like Bill. But it won't happen. We'll remain friends. Still, he gives me the key to his bungalow. "Whenever you guys come up, just stay here," he says.

Hours later, as we drive back to Laguna, I realize that on these little sojourns I am starting to feel myself again. And I am always a little crestfallen on the ride home. I keep the pad beside me and write down the vanity license plates I see. I look at the little pad. MSNLNKH. I still haven't figured that one out. Then I look at it again and laugh. Missing link. This place is funnier than I thought. I wonder what my vanity plate should read. TK RISKS sounds about right.

I make all sorts of mental notes about what I'm going to do when we get home. Call a friend I haven't talked to in a while, plan a new writing project, cook something I've never tried. I'm thinking of what I'll make for supper, when I notice the red brake lights ahead. Suddenly it's bumper to bumper as far as I can see. I don't know any side roads, other ways to head home. I put the radio on loud and tell Kate we'll just have to be patient.

Luckily I don't have anywhere to be, but what if I did? A friend who plays for the Los Angeles Philharmonic tells me that being stuck in traffic is no longer an excuse for missing a rehearsal. What makes me most anxious about this city is that you can never plan how long it will take you to get somewhere. In New York the subway takes thirty minutes to get me from my house to Penn Station; I can pretty much count on that. But traffic here is a great variable and almost impossible to predict.

There once was a mass transit system proposed for Los Angeles. In some parts of the city you can still see the rudimentary tracks. But in the 1920s it was purchased by a private citizen, who made it his goal to dismantle them. That man was Henry Ford. If Los Angeles is anything, it is the city born of the automobile and water. Compare this to New York, which grew up because of its port, or Chicago, which became a city in part because of its logistical setting of Fort Dearborn, at the mouth of the Chicago River, and Lake Michigan.

But Los Angeles came out of something else. A dreamer's dream, dismantled tracks, diverted water. It is not for nothing that film noir comes out of this place, that we cannot think of it without thinking of its slightly criminal, slightly underworld side.

New York has the mob and Chicago the political bosses, but Los Angeles has its municipal corruption. Who owns the water, who owns the roads? If *Chinatown* is the Los Angeles film about water, *Who Framed Roger Rabbit?* is the film about mass transit and the freeway system. It is set in a time when Los Angeles still had mass transit, known as the Red Car. In the film, Red Car has been bought by a private concern, Cloverleaf, whose goal is to build freeways. Its vision is of a city of gas stations, auto-parts shops, and fast-food restaurants, of cars driving on and off the freeway ramps all day long. As the evil Doon says at the end to Valiant, the private investigator, "I bought the Red Car so I could dismantle it." Doon is part of the takeover of Toontown, which will turn Los Angeles from a community into a postmodernist nightmare whose central image might well be the traffic jam, such as the one in which I now find myself.

We inch along for almost an hour until we reach the problem, a rear-ender in the express lane. Some driver must have tailgated another, who was driving too slowly. Rubberneckers snake their way around the smashup, where the police have just arrived. No one seems hurt.

Then the lanes open up. Traffic breezes along as if there haven't been any delays.

One Sunday I venture east. It is a road I haven't traveled on, Interstate 15, heading to Nevada. I pass Barstow, drive through Summit. I know I should turn around, but I keep driving. Where am I going? I ask myself, but I drive farther and farther into the Mojave.

Pink alkali flats take on shapes. As I drive, I think I see caravans, a village, herds gathering on the hills. A golden lake shimmers before me, but as I approach, it turns to sand. Except for the passing truckers and ghost towns where men sit on porches sipping beer, tattoos snaking up their arms, this desert is all mirages. I drive for hours, my forearm resting on the open window, the sun searing my skin.

In the rearview mirror I see Kate, asleep in her car seat, a rim of sweat on her brow, a thin coating of dust on her cheeks, as if she is another apparition. If I stop, she'll wake up, so I keep going, farther into the Mojave, which stretches like a blanket of yellow, red, lavender, in all directions.

The last gas station was an hour, two hours back. Maybe it was open, maybe it wasn't. The gas gauge hovers just above the red danger zone. I should have stopped then, but I didn't. I don't know how to change a tire or what to do if the radiator overheats. Whom I'll flag down for gas.

All I have with me is a jug of warm water, a blanket, and the CB radio my brother sent me when I moved west, which sits in the trunk, never installed. A voice tells me that none of this is a good idea, but still I keep moving. The radio plays "Mama, Don't Let Your Babies Grow Up to Be Cowboys," but I lose the station in midsong. Kate starts to fuss, and I'm feeling the heat as well.

Just across the Nevada border I pull over at a marriage chapel. This one is called "The Hitching Post," and I like its name. It has a soda machine and a gas pump and offers weddings twenty-four hours a day, no blood test. The A-frame of polyurethaned logs has a front porch, where Kate and I sit after I fill the tank, paying the boy who seems to have appeared out of nowhere.

On the porch is an outdoor altar with a bald eagle, a *faux* mountain backdrop, a dream catcher. Kate winces as I wipe her face with a Wash'n Dri. I give her a bottle of juice and put coins in the soda machine, which sells Dr Pepper in bottles. Peering inside the chapel, I see a small altar and Jesus, bleeding, a mournful look on his face, on the cross.

A couple arrives, wearing cowboy boots and Stetsons, jeans. Their witness is drunk and staggers along behind them. He invites us to join them. It's the third time they're marrying each other, the witness says. "Just Married Again" is painted on the side of their van. Kate and I move in closer as they knock on the door of a shack, waking the minister. He comes to the door, rubbing his eyes, and a few moments later emerges with a Bible and wearing a white shirt. Money is exchanged, and they opt for the outdoor Native American altar.

The ceremony is quick. If you blink, you've missed it. Kate reaches into the green Tupperware container, hurling rice a little too soon, hitting the minister in the eye. I sip my Dr Pepper as the couple give a holler, then stagger back to their car, kicking up dust with their heels. They wave and honk as they head west, full of dreams.

Twenty-one

A student of mine, Patricia Holland, has a strange story to tell. She was a second-grade teacher, and her classroom (like mine) was in a trailer. One day a little girl got up to ask Patricia a question, and Patricia, who was standing against the blackboard, felt a sudden searing pain race through her arm and she fell to the floor. Her arm, she saw, was ripped open and bleeding. Through the desk where the girl had been sitting just moments before there was a bullet hole.

Two hunters, a mile away, were having target practice against some rocks. A bullet ricocheted off the rocks, zoomed down the mountain and through the classroom window, then penetrated the seat of the little girl, who would have been killed if she hadn't gotten up to ask a question, and struck Patricia in the arm. She hasn't been in an elementary classroom since; instead she decided to go back to college. As she tells me this story, Patricia moves her arm to show me how it doesn't really bend.

Patricia starts to hang out at my office, to wait for me after school. She has a little boy named Jake, and one afternoon she comes by and our children play together. Patricia is a good writer and she is older than my other students. She is strong and enjoys hiking in the woods. Also, she is recovering from the trauma of a lawsuit, and since we both seem to be recovering from traumas, we like to spend time together.

"I don't know how you do it," she says as we put the kids in backpacks and hike up in the hills behind my house. "I couldn't do it without Joe."

"Well, I have help. . . ."

"It's not the same." Patricia shakes her head. She has reddish curls, freckles, a turned-up nose, and sturdy legs. She also has eight brothers and sisters and a father who reads novels in the living room with a martini beside him and all the kids running around. "I just don't think I could do it on my own."

I sigh. "I'm not sure I'm doing such a great job."

She gives Kate a tickle under her chin. "Oh, you seem to be doing all right."

"Sometimes I lose my temper. . . ."

"Sometimes we all do."

Patricia has a place up on Mono Lake, near Yosemite. As she describes freezing glacial lakes, meadows of wildflowers, Ansel Adams scenery, I can almost feel the cool waters, smell the mountain breeze. "Before you leave California, Mary, you'll have to come."

"Leave California?" I ask her, as if this thought never occurred to me before.

"Oh, were you planning to stay?" I was, I tell her. It was my plan. She shakes her head, taking this in. "I don't think you will."

Angie lays stones across my head, on my sinuses, along my brow. Brazilian agate for my physical stamina, green chrysoprase to balance my neurotic patterns, ease depression. A little clear quartz for vision, for wisdom without distortion. She burns cedar incense to clear my head and plays Native American chants to focus my energy. Massage is only a small part of what Angie does. Though I've come for the massage, I'm becoming fascinated with the stones.

Aquamarine will augment my power. Amazonite will help perfect my personal communication. I do not believe a word of this, but I like the feel of the smooth stones on my forehead, across my brow, on my sternum. "I'm rebalancing your energy," Angie says.

Just rub my back, I want to say, but the truth is, she is cheap (only thirty-five dollars an hour) and it feels good. Angie knows people who can help me. They can help with whatever ails you. "I know a lot of people who work with goddesses. I know a lot of psychics."

"What kind of psychics?"

"Oh, there's all kinds around here. Most psychics specialize these days. My friend Victoria Looseleaf, she goes to the psychic of bad teeth."

"Victoria Looseleaf?"

"Oh, she's a writer. That's an assumed name."

I nod and feel Angie dig into my ribs. "What does a psychic of bad teeth do?"

"Helps you manifest new ones. But he can't do crowns. Only new teeth."

"You're kidding."

Angie shakes her head and works my flesh like clay. "I wouldn't kid about something like that."

"What other kinds of psychics are there around here?"

"Oh, there's the psychic of unfinished tasks. He helps you finish things. And the psychic of lost objects. He helped a friend of mine find bearer bonds he'd misplaced. And there's the psychic of lost dogs."

"What does he do?"

"Well, the one I know about is a woman. She helps you find your dog if it's lost."

"Not cats?"

"Only dogs," Angie says with a smile.

"I don't have a dog."

"Well," Angie says, heating some suction cups, "I guess you won't have to call her. Now turn over." On my back she places the suction cups, which sizzle and burn against my skin.

Just before Christmas, a Santa Ana blows in from the desert, with winds up to sixty miles an hour. Trees come down. Sagebrush blows up and down the canyon road. Wind chimes in Laguna ring like wild. This is the time when there are more car accidents and suicides than at any other in Southern California. When the pyromaniacs like to set fires that sweep through the mountains.

I am invited for dinner at the home of my friend Catherine's stepfather. He lives with a woman named Betty in a trailer park. As I drive through Swan Lake Park, everything is decorated for Christmas. Outdoor lights act like strobes in the wind. Jesus songs play on the radio. Inside the trailer, which is warm and cozy, we eat paella and sip a very sweet sangria.

I met Catherine in Mexico over a decade ago. We traveled together. Then went our separate ways. But upon returning to the States we became fast friends. Now Catherine has come from New York to live with her mother in Costa Mesa for a few months and write her dissertation.

After dinner Catherine and I take a walk along the windy road. Sagebrush blows past us, and she asks me how I'm doing. "I suppose I've been better," I say. "He's coming here for Christmas." She has seen me through the whole relationship with Jeremy, and she knows I'm still hoping to work things out with him.

"Well, are you happy about that?"

"I think I am." Branches, leaves, whirl all around us. It is a strange, warm wind.

"You know," she says, "an acquaintance of mine introduced me to a friend of hers, a woman who lives in a nice house in Newport Beach. This woman is a kept woman. She is kept by a very famous, wealthy man. When you go over to her house, all the pictures are turned to the wall so you can't see his face. No one can know who this man is. He phones her three times a day—in the morning at about ten, at lunchtime, and in the evening. She has to be home for his calls. She's never quite sure when he might phone, so she only goes out for a few hours at a time. When I met her, she kept looking at her watch."

"Why are you telling me this?" I ask Catherine, irritation rising in my throat.

We have to step over a tree trunk that lies across the road. "I was just thinking you should get out more."

Twenty-two

When I met Jeremy, I was considering applying to law school. Or film school. Or moving back to the Midwest. That has always been on my mind. Moving home. I had had some success as a short story writer, but the publication of my first novel hadn't gone as I'd hoped, and shortly thereafter a man I thought I loved (or who at least met all the criteria on paper that seemed right) left me. Then Gabriel, the Cambodian spy who wanted me to read his manuscript, introduced me to Jeremy on the train platform.

We began to see each other for lunch at the faculty club. We ate and he made me laugh. He told very funny stories at other people's expense, hilarious stories about his colleagues, who often were sitting just a few tables over. He had a way of looking askew at the world. When people saw me with him, they asked me if I knew whom I was having lunch with. I really didn't.

"You know, he's very famous," the chair of my program said. "That's the man who proved the war in Vietnam was illegal," someone else said. I had had my involvements with sixties activists before. I'd worked at Beacon Press after college, and for a while we were hiding the Berrigans in our offices. Ray Mungo arrived in an elf suit to meet with Robert Redford. Daniel Ellsberg slipped a copy of the Pentagon papers to my boss, Arnold Tovel, and we worked around the clock, Xeroxing them, getting them ready to go to press. Once, I walked into an office at Beacon where Ellsberg was on the phone, and I heard him say, "Hi, Dad, it's me. I just want to tell you to watch CBS. I'll be on tonight. Oh, and did you see *Time*?" Another well-known peace activist was having an affair with my downstairs neighbor, and I'd always know when he'd paid her a visit, because she'd be dancing in her room like a ballerina when he left.

"Is he married?" I asked Frances once.

"Of course he's married," she replied.

I remember being confused then, during the sixties, about how these men could preach public morality, then cheat on their wives. Public good and private whatever.

A few weeks after we met, Jeremy phoned and asked me to go out to dinner. I told him I couldn't, because I was having dinner with Gabriel. "So meet me for a drink instead." Over drinks Jeremy made me laugh. I glanced at my watch. It was almost seven, but Jeremy said it was all right to be a little late; besides, he had to leave by seven-thirty. So I stayed and talked and laughed until seven-thirty, when I tore myself away, my head rolling with laughter—about what, I can't even recall. Even as I walked to the restaurant, I was laughing.

When I walked into the restaurant, nearby, Gabriel was eating dinner. He glanced at his watch. "You're late," he said without looking up at me.

"I'm sorry," I told him, my head still filled with the laughter I now had to contain. "Actually I was having drinks with Jeremy."

That didn't seem to make an impact. Gabriel didn't speak with me much through the meal, and after that he said goodbye. I never saw him again. Jeremy never saw him again either. The spy drifted back to wherever he'd come from. It was strange that he just disappeared. Later, when Jeremy and I were in Tortola or Amsterdam or somewhere, I asked him if he ever saw Gabriel, and Jeremy replied, "Don't you know, he was an angel. That was his whole purpose. He brought us together; then he went away."

Jeremy was a soft-spoken man. He never raised his voice. He never lost his temper. He spoke so softly I had to lean forward to listen. I had grown up with something else. Something I thought I was getting away from. Not only did my father have a temper, but he'd had scarlet fever as a boy and had only forty percent hearing. So even if he wasn't angry, it always sounded as if he was.

I'm not sure why the things that made him angry did so. Like lights being left on or the garage door open. But he is a very exacting man. He wants things just right, his own way. In another world he would have been a musician, but he had to earn a living for his family—first his brothers and parents, then us. Since he was nineteen, my father supported someone. It took its toll. In most ways my father is a good, kind man, given to crying at movies. I love talking to him on the phone. I love listening to his stories. But he is a temperamental man, and his children had to learn to negotiate his moods.

Sometimes we had a good time. I remember once we rented a boat and had fried chicken on the Fox River. My father steered the boat and kept calling, "Mark seagull on right," and we laughed at that because the gull always flew away. But mostly I remember how mad he got. It wasn't ever big things that set him off. Those he was quiet about, like when my brother brought home a bad report card or when someone had hurt one of us. It was about the house. About order. About things being the way he liked them. But no matter what, because of his deafness, my father never spoke. He shouted. He shouted for us to pass the salt or put our napkins in our laps. He shouted for us to clear the table or do our homework.

He shouted because he couldn't hear, and we had to shout back. When I think of my childhood, I think of this shouting. When I was sixteen my father had surgery. A bone was replaced in his ear, and tissue was supposed to grow over it. We were sitting in the living room one day, and my mother walked through the room. My father jumped into the air. "What was that?" he asked, his voice trembling in fear.

"It's footsteps, Daddy," I told him. He'd never heard them before. The world of sound was new to him. He heard train wheels. He'd always assumed his commuter train was silent before. He heard whispers, people talking behind his back. But mostly he heard our voices. That was something new. I didn't have to shout at my father to make myself heard. But he continued to shout at us. Not as much as before, but he shouted when things weren't right.

One day when I was in college, I'd gone to visit friends in the suburbs and was late for dinner. When I walked in, the table was cleared, dinner was gone. "Have you eaten already?" I asked. And my father yelled at me. He yelled very articulately. He sounded very smart. To this day, when someone yells at me or I'm angry with someone, I stammer. I can barely make myself understood.

But he stood up and yelled, and I cowered. Then my brother got up and stood in front of my father, arms folded across his chest. My brother raised a finger. He said, "You will never yell at her like that again." My father backed down. And he never did yell at me again.

So when Jeremy spoke so quietly that I had to lean close to listen, I thought this must be good. I must be safe.

• • •

I began seeing Jeremy more frequently for lunches. He wore a wedding ring. I knew he had two young boys. But I was seeing him for lunches, that's all. And he seemed really to listen to me. It was this ability he had, part of his Zen training. To be utterly in the present. When he was with you, he was totally with you. The corollary to this had not yet become apparent to me, though it would soon enough.

"I'm going to law school," I told him. "I'm going to do something else with my life."

He shook his head, bemused. "Why don't you think about it for a while?" he said.

During fall break, my mother and I had a long-scheduled trip to make to London and France. Jeremy was going around the world. Before he left, I pressed into his hand a copy of my first collection of short stories.

My mother and I flew to Paris, where we walked the Champs Élysées, trying to recapture a visit we'd made there when I was fifteen, some twenty years before, looking for the peach melba we'd once savored at the Hôtel Vendôme, for that little bistro in Montmartre that the tourists hadn't discovered back then. It was a miserable trip for me because, though I did not want this to be the case, though I tried and fought against my better nature, though I loved my mother, I was traveling with the wrong person. I knew the person I belonged with was Jeremy.

We were walking down the Champs Élysées one afternoon, and as my mother paused to look at perfume bottles in a store, a Gypsy in a ratty fake-fur coat pulled me aside and read my palm. "You are falling in love with an older man," she told me. "He is married, but he will leave his wife, and you will be happy for the rest of your life." I stared at the woman in disbelief. After all, a fortune-teller had predicted my parents' marriage. I have read palms now for many years, and I believe that the Gypsy who pulled me aside on that Paris street saw what she said she saw. It was as if her words sealed my fate.

Jeremy called me as soon as we were home. "You know, I misread those blue midwestern eyes," he told me. "You've got eyes like an innocent, but now I've read your book and I know you aren't one."

"I'm giving it up. I'm going to do something else with my life," I told him again.

"You don't know your destiny," he said.

I was stunned the first time I saw his house—a beautiful old colonial with modern built-ins, every wall lined with bookshelves, piles of papers everywhere, the dining room table buried under newspapers, bills, letters, manuscripts, the bedroom littered with papers, the dresser covered in foreign money, one chair with a month's worth of dirty laundry sitting on it.

When he took me to his house at night, I'd sit in the television room while he had long, rambling whispered phone conversations with his wife and other conversations that seemed more whispered and more secretive, which did not seem to be with his wife. I saw him, leaning over the counter, hand on his head, trying to speak as softly as he could in an already soft-spoken voice. "Who is it?" I asked when he was off the phone. "Who are you talking to?"

"It's just complications," he said, "things I need to take care of."

Then I made him drive me back to the makeshift accommodations where I stayed those nights when I was teaching and, therefore, in town.

One night he asked me to stay with him. He came downstairs

wearing a red dashiki, which looked ridiculous, and said, "Please spend the night."

"Not if you're still married. Not until you've separated from your wife."

But still, on Wednesday nights when I was at the university, I went to that rambling house of books and papers, his wife living mainly in New York with the boys. The layers of his life became revealed to me slowly. While he was on the phone, I tried to create order—stacking the newspapers in neat piles, sorting through the bills, carting clothes down to the washing machine. Once or twice I picked up the phone, wanting to check my machine. I heard women speaking in soft Indian accents, Australian accents, a voice from Scandinavia.

Later, when he came upstairs, I asked, "Tell me, just how complicated is your life?"

"It's going to be a lot less complicated in a few weeks," he said, giving me a peck on the cheek.

By Christmas he had left his wife. By January, over the midwinter break, we flew to Tortola. We rented a house and stayed there half the day, reading, writing, making love. By midday we headed to the beach, and at night we danced to the conga drums. Every day or so I said to him, "Don't you think you should call home? Talk to your kids?"

He'd shake his head. He told me it was better for them if they didn't hear from him for a while. "But they're little, aren't they?" I said. I once caught a glimpse of Evan, who was eleven at the time, in front of the Regency Hotel, a dark-haired boy with a big smile. "Don't you think you should give your boys a call?"

"I'll call when I'm home," Jeremy said.

We had a wonderful, perfect time in Tortola. Then, as soon

as we were back in New York, Jeremy began traveling again. On weekends, he was in Amsterdam, Mexico City, The Hague, Iceland, Vancouver—I can't remember where. Weekends when he wasn't traveling, he had his boys or he had unexpected guests from out of town, with whom he had to write position papers or resolve legal problems. Once in a while on a weekend I'd ramble around his house, while downstairs men with beards or turbans or women with thick Irish accents or antinuclear activists from England stayed up with Jeremy until all hours, drinking wine, discussing their particular causes. Who was I to object to these meetings, who was I to beg him to come to bed?

I learned to play tennis. I was surprisingly good at it, briefly. I got a coach, and one of Jeremy's boys hit balls with me. I revived a two-fisted backhand that I could slam anywhere on the court. I learned to read the newspaper cover to cover and sat through two quarters of a Sunday football game. I made platters of roast beef sandwiches. I cooked. But for some reason it seemed as if I was always alone.

On the weekends when he was traveling, he phoned me from all over the world. I'd be in my New York apartment with my cat, waiting for his calls. Often at night I drank. Vodka or brandy to put me to sleep, cigarettes to calm my nerves. I'd never needed to do this before. I turned down dates, refused friends, just to stay home in case Jeremy called. I missed movies, dinner, the opera, so as not to miss his calls. Sometimes when he called, I told him I was lonely, that I missed him. "Do you have to go away all the time?"

"So many people need me, but I'm going to cut back, I promise. I want to be with you," was what he always said.

One weekend when the airfare was cheap, I went with him to Amsterdam. We flew over, checked into a good hotel, then spent a day strolling the canals, going to museums, eating *rijsttafel.* The next morning we moved to a dingy room in the hotel where his conference on disarmament was being held, and for two days I walked the canals.

I went to the Van Gogh Museum, where I stared at *Irises*, at *Vincent's Bedroon in Arles*. I looked at van Gogh's thick, heavy brush strokes, those deep, wild swirls, and thought about what it takes to make a person go insane. I kept going back and looking at these paintings, over and over again.

Twenty-three

Wanda phones to say that Ashtar will speak through her on Friday night at Visions and Dreams bookstore. He asked specifically that I attend. Well, it was nice of him to invite me, I say, but Wanda doesn't laugh. Sure, I reply, recovering quickly, I'll be there. I ask Ramona to stay until Saturday morning, and she agrees.

On Friday night I make my way to Visions and Dreams, where an upstairs room is partially full, mainly with women, some of them quite obese. The women, who have come to listen to what Ashtar has to say, look glum and stolid, and as I take a seat on a folding chair near the back, no one speaks or smiles. We are quiet until Wanda walks in.

She greets us in her warm, friendly manner, and everyone

nods solemnly. Asking that the lights be dimmed, she announces that Ashtar will soon arrive. Her eyes closed, Wanda goes into one of her light trances. Then Ashtar begins to speak. It is a long, rambling speech, spoken in that high-pitched, almost robotic voice.

You have not honored your growth, he begins. You are still involved in the game of looking for something outside yourself to fulfill the self. But you are the masters of yourselves and all that exists within you. Now you need not look any further. It is within you. Yet you fear looking within and seeing yourself. What are you afraid of seeing? Your anger, your fear? Is it possible you have forgotten who you are?

Humanity is an isolated consciousness, separated from the light, rejected by the light, by the divinity. Earth is a level of punishment. Why must we live in this physical body? It dies, gets disease. What is the use of this skin bag if you can fly, levitate, transmute? Perhaps some of you have gained weight. This is the body's attempt to ground you, to hold you back. It is the body's fear of transcendence, of change. But you must not resist change. Your mission here is simple. You are to help prepare the earth and therefore yourselves for her limitlessness and for your own. We are here to help the earth remember. My command, my light vehicles, which circle the earth, are here to enable you to achieve your potential before departing from the planetary plane.

Below the earth's surface there are many etheric centers where extraterrestrials are working underground. In these centers are pockets of dense energy, which is being released. The earthquakes and aftershocks we have been experiencing recently are all part of that shift in the earth's consciousness.

None who sit here is originally from the planet earth. Our loneliness, the isolation we feel, is because we are light beings stuck within the limitations of the body and the third dimension.

You are the medium through which this New Age will come to the earth. You are the gods in disguise. You have been chosen to heal, to remember. You have been chosen so that you may fully become the light that shines within you.

Perhaps you feel as if you are not at home, you are away from home. What you need to know is that everything that passes through you is home. You are at home in the self.

Death Valley

Twenty-four

En route to Death Valley, we drive through Summit, the pass many making the trek west in 1849 could not cross. Jeremy drives, and I stare out the window as the desert zips past. I love the names of the roads—Wild Wash Road, Victory in Jesus, Ghost Town Road. A Century 21 sign is stuck in the middle of the desert, in the middle of nowhere. We pass the Apache Trading Post, which offers twenty-four-hour towing and warns that the next service station is fifty-seven miles away.

We stop at Hillbilly Burger, where there is a kind of jar on our table and, sitting on top of it, a small statue of a turbaned man in a loincloth. A sign at the little man's feet says, "Ask the Swami." Is my future bright? Should I take a vacation? Does he/she love me? I put in a quarter, and the swami lights up, spins around, then spits out a piece of paper. "The heart knows what the mind neglects," my slip of paper reads. Some swami, I say, biting into my burger.

We push on. Ahead of us are emerald mountains, mud rising like elephants' backs, an unreal landscape of black lava hills, sulfur springs, dried desert holly. As we head into Death Valley, a map shows the way to Zabriskie Point, Dante's View. We reach the lowest point in the United States—282 feet below sea level—and it is like being at the bottom of a dried-up ocean. I recall *Death Valley Days* and Twenty Mule Team Borax. It all seems entirely plausible.

There are little deaths here. The death of longing, for one. Jeremy and I have dinner, the golden-red desert stretching outside the window. Just make a decision, I ask him. I want to know what you want. "Of course I want you," he replies. "I'm here, aren't I?" Yes, he is here. He spent Christmas with his boys, then came two days later. That must count for something, I try to tell myself.

"Everything will work out," he tells me, "if you could just stop making demands." His voice rises, and for the first time I detect a twinge of impatience, of anger, in it.

"But why not just say yes?" I argue. "Why not just try?"

"You wanted this baby," he tells me, as if I need to be reminded. "This was your choice."

"But you knew I was trying to have a child."

As always, it ends in a stalemate. Jeremy, who has a joint degree in law and Eastern philosophy from Yale, tells me once again that I need to let go in order to have. I tell him that I need to pay my bills and raise my daughter. We sleep chastely side by side. I have no desire to touch or be touched. I attribute this to motherhood, to nursing, and not to revulsion or fear. I do not know that I am protecting myself. Even this small journey away from her makes my body ache, hurts me. If I long for anything, it is for her.

On the way to Nevada, the radio plays "Rhinestone Cowboy." We pause for a drink at the Waterhole Saloon, play the slots. Near the state line we pass Whiskey Pete's, which is across the street from Kactus Kate's. Back at the Waterhole, I saw signs that a seven-year-old boy, Alexander Harris, disappeared inside Whiskey Pete's. He was taken by a stranger, and the man in the poster looked like your generic bad man—dark pants, dark shirt, dark glasses, cap on his head. Later Alexander Harris will be found dead, not far from the saloon.

I panic at this notice, tell Jeremy I want to go home. But we are already near Vegas. "Do you really want me to turn around?"

"Yes," I say, my voice thick with irony. "I want you to want to turn around." He doesn't get it. He starts to make a U-turn, and I tell him, "It's all right; keep going." I settle back, missing Kate, trying not to think of her. She's all right, I tell myself. She'll be fine. The Mojave, with its heat and colors, lulls me into a hypnotic trance. I close my eyes, let the wind hit my face.

We cross into Nevada and pass Outpost Junction, where there is a sign for instant weddings, twenty-four hours, no blood test required. "Why don't we stop?" I ask Jeremy, and he laughs at my joke.

By evening we reach the hills above Vegas, where the red lights shimmer, like Bethlehem. Vegas was Bugsy Siegel's dream in the Mojave. He got in his car in Los Angeles one day, drove into the desert, and stopped right where the Strip is today. I'm going to make a new city here, Siegel said. Like something out of the Bible. Everyone thought he was crazy like Moses, wandering the desert, a vision in his head. He envisioned the Flamingo and lived to see it built, though not to reap its benefits, for he was killed, execution style, in June 1947, just weeks after I was born.

It is more like Sodom, I think, as we drive through town. I am stunned by Caesars, the Ali Baba, the Dunes. Marriage chapels are everywhere. A water-bed honeymoon is thrown in. One chapel offers an airplane with two hundred eighty-five lights to announce your intentions. There is a photographic sample on the wall. "Dear Paula, Wanted it to be unique and now it is. Will you marry me?"

We check into Bally's and hit the tables. Blackjack, I'm told, is a system game, and if you play it right, you can win. But no one tells me the system, and I lose two hundred dollars I don't have in a matter of minutes. The dealer asks if I want to play again, but I shake my head. Jeremy plays more thoughtfully, but pretty soon he's down as well. He laughs it off; to him, it's not that much to lose.

Afterward we take in a show—dancing girls, tigers, some magic tricks. In the morning we're on the road.

The afternoon of New Year's Eve we are back in Laguna. Somehow Ramona has sensed we are coming, because she's out in the yard with Kate in her arms, waiting for us. When we pull up, I sweep my daughter into my arms. She's dressed for a holiday, in a red-and-white cotton print. Ramona is heading off to a party, and she's all dressed up as well, ready to go when we arrive. I won't see her for three days.

She was going to go and get her son during the holidays, but in the end she decided to wait until she had more money saved. She has been squirreling away whatever I give her, and in a few months she'll get him. Though she hasn't asked, I know she wishes I'd lend her the money to bring him back, but as it is, I'm living paycheck to paycheck. I can't bear to think of the two hundred I dropped in Vegas, money that would easily have brought her son here.

Whenever she can, Ramona wants to get out of the house. I don't blame her. She does her work, but then she's ready to leave. "Okay," she says, almost as soon as our car pulls up. "I'm leaving." She wishes us Happy New Year, then she's gone.

After she leaves, I cut Jeremy's hair, which has grown wild and scruffy since we were last together in October. "You should go to a barbershop," I tell him, "especially when we're apart like this."

He clasps my hand as the scissors flies. "We just have to see each other more."

"How much more?" I ask, his hair falling onto the patio in silver-gray clumps. I am moving on to the beard.

He turns, taking the scissors out of my hand. "Maybe a lot more." We order in take-out Chinese and, after Kate falls asleep, snuggle up on the couch to watch a movie on TV. Just after midnight the phone rings. I look at Jeremy and shrug, then go and answer it.

A woman's voice, foreign and far away, asks for Jeremy. "Who is this?" I say, but I don't wait for an answer. The foreign voice bumbles on the other end. I give him a look, tell him it's for him. He takes it in the kitchen, then leans over the counter, resting on his elbows. His voice is barely a whisper. I've seen him in this stance before.

He stands hunched in my kitchen, whispering into the phone as he did soon after we met, and I go into Kate's room and grab a pillow and blanket off Ramona's bed. He sees me dragging the bedding into the living room. Quickly he gets off the phone. "What is your problem?" he asks me. He says he barely knows her.

"So how did she get my number?"

His secretary must have given it out inadvertently. It is a mistake, he assures me. Nothing I should feel threatened by. She's somewhere in Australia. She just wanted to wish him Happy New Year. Just some woman he met at a conference.

"But the voice was familiar to me," I tell him.

"Well, it shouldn't be," he says. He looks glumly at the sofa, where I have made up his bed. I relent, but still, for so long now I can barely remember, we do not touch.

New Year's Day, I am bone-tired. Jeremy and I both have work to do, papers to grade, but I tell him I must take a nap. "Can you watch Kate?"

He promises he will, and I fall into a deep slumber. As I sleep, I have this dream: I come to a house, not so different from the bungalow, and there are many strange machines. Machines that wash your walls, open your mail. The person who lives here has left me twenty-seven houseplants, which require constant care. Throughout the dream I rush around, watering them. The house has no plumbing, no pipes. Water pours everywhere, flooding wherever I turn. Several dark men in bathing suits walk around, saying there is no sun. There won't be any for weeks.

I wake, shaken by the darkness of the dream, wondering what it means, and stagger, bleary-eyed, into the living room, where I find Jeremy, his eyes glued to the Rose Bowl game. "Where's the baby?" I ask him. He looks up, gives me a blank stare, then his gaze flickers about the room. *"Where is she?"*

I chase around the bungalow, find her in the dining room, her tiny finger poking curiously at an electrical socket. I recall the last session of the Lamaze classes I attended with my friend Michael and without Jeremy. The baby safety class. What do you do if your baby is on fire? Throw a blanket over her. What do you do if your baby is plugged into an electrical socket? Hit her with a broom. I'd begun to laugh over these admonitions, and Michael had to shush me.

Now, scooping Kate into my arms, I press her to me, then race back into the living room. *"How could you?"* I shout at him. Jeremy glances at me, one eye still on the Rose Bowl game. From the shrieks of the crowd, I can tell that some startling play has just occurred. "I asked you to watch her. How could you?"

"It was only for a second. I just took my eyes away for a second."

"That's all it takes," I say.

I grab the baby, and suddenly I am afraid for her. Not that she could have put her finger into a socket, but afraid for something deeper. Something I can't quite name. But I know I must protect her in ways I hadn't imagined before.

Twenty-five

Wanda lives in an apartment house in the outskirts of Anaheim, not far from Disneyland. I drive past apartment buildings, fast-food chains, a generic strip. Dazzled by the lights and the traffic, I am late as usual. Wanda called me a few nights ago to say that Ashtar wanted to assemble a special gathering of his earth-based unit. There was a ten-dollar charge, but for that we would all become intergalactic seeders, creating cosmic light centers, connecting all New Age Workers. Wanda told me that Ashtar assured her the light workers would be the first aboard the starships when the end of the world occurs.

Like early boarding, I wanted to say, for first class and people traveling with small children. But I resisted the joke. Wanda gave me her address, the date and time, and I said I'd be there.

The night of the meeting, I leave late, drive too fast. As I travel to Anaheim, I'm out of sorts. Nothing seems to be going right, and Jeremy's visit has left me uneasy. On the freeway, a car cuts me off. For the first time, I think: What if something happened to me; what would become of Kate? I try to envision Jeremy raising her, and I cannot. I wish I had a crystal ball and could see what the future holds. I wish I knew if everything was going to be all right.

I have trouble finding the place and drive through the streets of Anaheim until I come to a brick housing complex with a few dozen cars parked out front. The ordinariness of this apartment building strikes me—no dramatic vistas, no quaint, peaceful village. Just fast food, heavily traveled roads, another generic strip, a housing complex from the early seventies.

Since I arrive late, the circle has already been formed. Strangers greet me with broad smiles. A space is made for me in a circle of crystals, where I am surrounded by books on dolphin communication, how to be your own best friend, Ramatha speaks. The decor looks like it comes from a Sears catalog, except that crystals are literally everywhere. Angels dangle overhead. A black cat named Midnight moves on white paws among the candles, never singeing its fur.

They have been waiting for me, Wanda says, and by "they" she means Ashtar and his fleet. They did not wish to join us until I was here. "Mary is often late," Wanda says. "That is because she has so much to do." She smiles at me, and for some reason I don't feel chided. Everyone inside the circle also smiles at me, and Wanda asks that we hold hands, creating an energy circle with which to welcome Ashtar.

In a matter of moments Wanda is in her light trance and Ashtar greets us. He tells us how we are his light workers, his intergalactic seeders, and that he has called us together to enable us to get in touch with our intergalactic power—not our spiritual power, not our ego potential, not our earthly capability, but our intergalactic power.

I gaze around the room. The participants seem normal enough. They wear jeans and polo shirts; they are well groomed, the men clean shaven. Ashtar wants us to introduce ourselves. Now that we will be working together, we must end our isolation and reach out of our solitary selves. We go around the circle. Carl, a nice-looking man with a mustache, is a muscular therapist; he says he's been waiting and preparing for this call all his life. Then Joseph—a handsome young black man with a radiant smile—who describes himself as a writer/entertainer, says that he, too, has been waiting for the call. A woman named Dawn, who runs a light center, keeps belching and farting, then falls asleep and snores. Lila, an astrologer, has brought her friend Caroline, an Asian crystal consultant and past-life regressor—which I first understand as transgressor.

Bob is a toymaker from Mattel, and Fred works for the government. Fred informs us that he has been abducted, taken to a planet where intelligent giant gray caterpillars rule. He says he enjoyed being with them on their planet, but they had no food, and he has been hungry ever since. We all nod sympathetically; no one seems to find this strange. There's a nutritionist whose name I don't get and Marcia, an interior decorator who makes wall hangings out of shells, coral, driftwood, bone, seaweed, natural objects. I introduce myself as a teacher and single parent.

Now that we know one another, Ashtar wants to welcome us as intergalactic seeders, members of the special fleet. We are invited to become members of the earth-based unit of the Ashtar command. Ashtar asks that we go around the circle and say what we believe we will gain by becoming intergalactic seeders. Carl, the muscular therapist, says he hopes he'll get more clients, and Marcia, the interior decorator, wants her work to be recognized. Joseph, the entertainer, is hoping for more gigs. When it is my turn, my mind draws a blank. I tell Ashtar I need time to think.

It seems as if everyone wants referrals, more clients, or consumers to buy their crystals or their books. They also are excited about participating in the great adventure and being the first light workers to board the spaceships when Armageddon comes. Then Wanda wants to inform us of what she'd like, and Ashtar suggests she speak for herself. Wanda leaves her trance and smiles at us.

She begins to speak in her normal voice. "I have always felt alone," she tells us. "I have lived alone and worked alone. But now

I feel it is time for me to reach out and try to get into contact, to network. I have never trusted humanity very much, and I'm not really much of a third-dimension person, but I feel I have come from another dimension and have never felt comfortable with earth beings. I have been sent to help from the earth-based unit of the Ashtar command. I have felt vulnerable and uncertain, like Midnight, my cat"—whom Wanda now reaches for and strokes. "I have been unsure of how you can trust being stroked. But now it is time to network. You can keep your own individuality," she informs us, "and still let go of your isolation."

We all nod and agree. "Hear! Hear!" a few muffled voices say. Then we join hands and close our eyes as Wanda blesses the newly formed earth-based unit and its mission.

Twenty-six

It is 1988, the end of the Reagan years, though four years of George Bush lie ahead. The Berlin Wall isn't down, but the cold war is ending. There's no other war for the moment. Springsteen is still the Boss, and the economy is recovering from the market crash last October, though trickle-down economics isn't working. Gary Trudeau's comic series "Where Is Reagan's Brain?" has circulated widely. The ozone layer is depleting; inside traders are the big news. O.J. hasn't happened. None of the American Gothic crimes of the early nineties has occurred. The music is heavy metal; the bonds are junk. The Los Angeles Dodgers will win the World Series.

Cosmically speaking, 1988 is considered an *eight* year in terms of numerology and tarot. 1 + 9 + 8 + 8 = 26. 2 + 6 = 8. Look at that number. It's balanced on the top and bottom. According to the Edenic Light Center newsletter, 1988 has no beginning and no end. It's a mirror of the balance and harmony we all seek in body, mind, and spirit. Gnosticism is experiencing a comeback. Meanwhile, UFO sightings are proliferating. Indeed, more UFO sightings occur in the American West than everywhere else in the world combined. Alien abductions are becoming the norm. Someone has mailed me the classified documents from Roswell, revealing where the extraterrestrial corpses are being kept.

My friend Bill sends me a chapter from *The Evolution of Civilizations,* by Carroll Quigley, published by Macmillan in 1961. In Chapter 5, entitled "Historical Change in Civilizations," Quigley discusses the seven phases in the evolution of civilization: mixture, gestation, expansion, conflict, universal empire, decay, invasion. America, he asserts, has expanded, and now we're in the conflict stage. After empire comes decay.

The end of an empire is often marked by superstition. This was true of ancient Greece; also Rome. The cold war is coming to an end. The millennium is ahead. We cannot fight Indians anymore. It's not PC. In two years there'll be the Gulf War, but everyone knows what to think about that. Westward expansion is no longer possible. War as we know it is dead. The enemy, if there is one, must be above. We don't have the wherewithal to look within. So we look up.

Or, as the French writer Joseph Jourbet wrote in 1784, "If the earth must perish, then astronomy is our only consolation."

When the phone rings at night, sometimes it's a student with a question about an assignment, sometimes it's my parents. I've made a few friends—an older couple from the university have taken me under their wing, and a few graduate students come over from time to time. But now when the phone rings, I do something I haven't done before. I screen my calls. Ramona doesn't like this, because her friends hang up on hearing the message tape, but I won't answer. I don't want to talk to Jeremy.

One day I sit and listen to him ramble on. "You're never there," he says. "You say you are so lonely, but you seem to be out all the time now. I never find you at home. Perhaps you are involved in a great creative endeavor. Perhaps you have met someone new, though I, of course, hope it is the former, not the latter. It's a beautiful day here. Sunny, warm. I played tennis for the first time since the fall. We could see our breath. I played very well. My serve has gotten quite strong. I have to go to Finland in February. I wish you could go with me. It would be lovely to sit with you in a little hotel in Helsinki."

I lean against the wall, listening. It takes all my strength not to pick up the phone.

Catherine comes over for dinner a few nights later and asks me what's going on with Jeremy. I tell her I'm not sure. "There was this phone call New Year's Eve. . . ."

"And who do you think was calling?"

"I don't know," I say.

"I do," Catherine says. "I'm sure it was Sigrid."

I try to remember the woman's voice, place her accent. "Whatever it was with Sigrid was over a long time ago. He told me that. He wouldn't lie to my face, would he?"

She ignores my question. "I'm sure it was Sigrid," Catherine insists. I am annoyed with her for saying that to me, for not minding her own business. I want to tell her this, but I'm afraid of losing my only friend within a fifty-mile radius.

That night as she leaves she tells me to be careful. "Watch your back," she says.

When Catherine goes home the phone rings, and I sit nursing the baby as Jeremy leaves another one of his endless messages on my machine. He offers to pay half my way to Finland. His tennis is better. The woman is no one; barely an acquaintance. Why don't we make Valentine's plans? Why don't I come home?

I'll make him wait. I'll answer when I'm good and ready. It gives me pleasure to hear him rambling on, but already I'm starting to break down. Still, depression settles in. I manage to complete the novel I've worked on for the past few years, but I know it's no good. I decide to forget about it. Instead of sending it to my agent, I place it in my desk, in a bottom drawer, where it will remain for the next six months.

A few nights later, a Saturday, Kate seems feverish. She tugs on her ears and whimpers. She won't rest except in my arms. I phone a doctor, but his service tells me that if this is an emergency, I should go to the hospital. I take her temperature. It isn't very high, but she appears to be in pain.

There is no one nearby. No one I can call. I give her a little Tylenol and rock her in my arms. Dozing in the chair, I wake up with her screaming, sobbing in my arms. Her fever has risen. I phone the doctor again, beg his service to get him to call me. I walk her, thinking I should take her to the emergency room, but she seems to settle back down again. When the doctor calls, he tells me to give her more Tylenol and call him in the morning.

I rock her until daybreak, when I see blood coming out of both ears. "Oh, my God," I cry. "Oh, my God." I phone the doctor, hysterical. "I'm taking her to the hospital." He says he'll meet me there.

I don't know what to do, whom to turn to. I phone my student

Patricia, but she isn't there. She must be at her place at Mono Lake. I try to think of whom else I can call, and in the end I just race to the emergency room, though Kate seems quieter now. The doctor has phoned ahead, and they take us in right away. She has a double ear infection, and her eardrums have burst. "Actually," the doctor says, "she'll be better now. She'll be all right." He gives me antibiotics and something for the pain. "Go home," he tells me. "Get some rest."

Home, I collapse with Kate on the sofa. Together we sleep for most of the day.

The Desert Mirage

Twenty-seven

When I don't know what else to do with myself, I drive. I pick up the 15 near San Bernardino, head toward Nevada, then turn right or left into the Mojave, onto one of those roads leading to nowhere that I first saw when the plane brought us here. Kate seems to like these drives with the wind on her face, the desert zipping by. I think to myself: This is dangerous, anything can happen; but I keep going.

In dried-up desert towns, I play the slots, order malted milks, which Kate and I sip in tandem at soda fountains. Then, when I can't stand it anymore, I phone Jeremy from phone booths in the middle of dusty fields. While Kate toddles around the booth, staring at me, her face and fingers pressed to the glass, I talk into his machine for as long as he talks into mine. I tell him I want to get married. I tell him I love him and we should try again.

In the middle of one of these calls he picks up. "I'm so glad to hear from you," he says.

"I miss you so much," I tell him. His voice is warm, lilting, like coming home, and I cannot pull myself away. In those phone booths in the middle of desert towns, I hear him tell me to be patient, to wait. He has finances to settle, his sons need to grow. He'll be ready to accept more responsibility soon. Sometimes I ask for money—not much, a little help—but he always sighs. He has so many demands on him. If I could just not add to them. He'll see me at Valentine's Day. I'll fly there. "I'm short of cash," I tell him.

"Put it on Sign and Travel," he says. "American Express."

In one of those towns, just after I've made such a phone call, a man with tattoos up and down his arms and beer bottles piled on his front porch offers to buy Kate. He says, "If you want, I'll trade this dog for her." He points to a mangy mongrel. The man laughs, taking a swig of his beer. He says he'll call it an even trade.

I get in the car and drive away with her as fast as I can, dust rising in my wake.

Twenty-eight

Some of the graduate students invite me to Los Angeles on a Friday evening to hear Spalding Gray at the Mark Taper Forum. Ramona agrees to stay with Kate. The students are going to be in the city that afternoon, and I'm to meet them at the Beverly Center at six o'clock for dinner. I give myself what seems like plenty of time: three hours to make the fifty-mile drive.

It is gray and rainy as I leave my house at three in the afternoon. I take Canyon Road and think as I pass Ralph's that maybe I should get my windshield wiper checked again, because it is raining. But it hasn't given me trouble in a while, and I don't want to be late. I breeze along on the 405. Traffic is light, and I think I'll be there in no time. Nothing to slow me down. The rain starts to fall a little more heavily. The road thickens with trucks, but I keep driving.

Then I notice the brake lights ahead. Cars are slowing down, but I don't think much of it. Now the rain comes down harder. I put on my defrost, turn up the radio. I switch on the wipers, and the one on the driver's side flips itself in the odd way and starts wiping the side of my car. Ahead of me, traffic has stopped moving.

It is gray all around. Driving rain, trucks, exhaust, and the windshield wiper scraping the body of my car. I cannot see a thing, but what I can see looks like something out of the seventh circle of hell.

It takes me four hours to get to the Beverly Center. My friends have left. I have no ticket and no time to get to Spalding Gray, nowhere else to go. I call an acquaintance from publishing, and he happens to be free. He takes me to a nearby bar and buys me dinner. We sit in a dark, smoky room and eat Thai food.

It's still pouring when we finish dinner, and no one can fix my windshield wiper until the next day, and my friend assures me it is not safe for me to drive home. He'd put me up, he says, but his place is so tiny. I phone my friend Bill, to see if I can stay there, but Bill isn't home, and I didn't think to bring his key. There's no one else I can think of imposing upon at this late hour, so further deepening my credit card debt, I check into the Shangri-La, where mysterious movie stars stay. This is much more money than I have to spend, but I do not think about it as, after calling Ramona, I slip into bed.

From between the cool white sheets in the bleached white room of the Shangri-La, where secrets are staunchly kept, I call Jeremy. I let the phone ring and ring, but there is no answer. I call back again, but not even the machine picks up.

In the morning I go to the Rose Café for breakfast. A man at the next table wears a body shirt and has a patch over his eye, a ring in his ear. A blue macaw sits opposite him, eating bananas off a fruit plate. A lovely old woman with flaming red hair greets strangers with an outstretched hand. "You remember me, darling, don't you?"

• • •

A friend from high school who wrote *Revenge of the Nerds* lives in Santa Monica, and the next weekend Kate and I go up there. Zach has three kids and a big backyard, and Kate falls in easily with their crowd. Zach's wife is an avid walker, so I tag along. "So," Marcia says, "do you like it here? A lot of Illinois people live here. We like it a lot, and Zach has this great job. . . ." Zach earns quite a bit of money, sitting in an office, writing scripts that probably won't get produced, though some will. "Anyway, it's home to us and we have a lot of friends. You must know Mark Victor."

I nod. I don't know him personally, but I knew his brother, Stuart. When I was twenty-two years old and in graduate school at Harvard, an old friend from Illinois came to visit. It was the Sunday of the solar eclipse, and everyone was out on the Charles River bank with smoky glass, waiting for the world to turn black in the middle of a sunny afternoon. On our way to see the eclipse, my friend and I stopped at an apartment in Cambridge where Debbie Schoen was said to live, but she wasn't home. Nor was her boyfriend, Stuart Victor, who was visiting Debbie that weekend.

Later we would learn that Stuart Victor was on Cape Cod with his estranged girlfriend, Debbie Schoen, whose brother was in my class. That afternoon, as the moon blotted out the sun, Stuart Victor killed Debbie Schoen, then took his own life.

As I visit with Marcia and Steve Zacharias, Marcia tells me the story of what happened in the Victor family after Stuart's murder and suicide. His parents could not comprehend what had led their son to commit this crime. Though he was said to be strange, he was also a handsome athlete, a boy girls were wild about. Rumor had it that he lived in a basement he had painted black, but in his darkness there was something that people were drawn to.

Marcia tells me how the Victors have been in contact with Stuart. They tried psychics all over the world, but finally they found a woman named Emma Twig, who lived in the backwoods in England and wouldn't take any money. The whole family, including Stuart's siblings, Mark and a sister, went together, trying to find Stuart and understand why he did what he did. They apparently made contact, and Mark asked Stuart what the food was like, and Stuart replied that one thing he couldn't stand was to see people eating.

Marcia says that for years the Victors kept up psychic contact, trying to achieve understanding. Lately, she says, Stuart has been slipping away. Now Mark feels that his brother has gone somewhere to rest. Mark has become quite successful in Hollywood. He wrote the movie *Poltergeist.*

"People will believe anything," I tell Marcia, thinking that I'm having enough trouble contacting the living.

"Why not?" Marcia says. "Why shouldn't they?"

The trumpet is blaring at Santa Anita. Flags are flying and it is a beautiful day as I make my way to the box Zach has taken seats in for our afternoon at the track. The horses are in the paddock, parading before the first race. Other Hollywood people are already in the box, including Jack Nietzch, the composer, Robert Downey, the director, plus assorted trainers, owners, money people, business managers, film people. The writers union is on strike, and with nobody working, people are betting.

No one is talking in the box. They are all poring over the racing pages. Robert Downey has a pencil behind his ear. They're all in jeans. The stakes are high. Zach hands me a racing form, and I can make no sense out of it. He suggests I go look at the horses in the paddock and see which ones appeal to me.

I watch the horses. There's a big black horse everyone says is the favorite and a chestnut colt they claim hasn't a prayer. But I like the way he kicks his heels. He fights back. His name is Dream Feathers, and I also like his name. His odds are fifteen to one. "Ten dollars on him to place," I tell Zach.

"Fat chance," Zach says.

"Is that a horse?" Robert Downey inquires, looking up from his racing form.

Zach puts a high bid on the first horse and assorted other bids on horse races in other states, in othe countries. He says he could just sit in a betting parlor and do this, but he likes to get out, see his friends, come to the track.

The horses are at the gate, the gun goes off. I watch them stream by, and then they're gone. Dream Feathers comes in second, and I walk away with a hundred and sixty. "Beginner's luck," Zach says when we cash in our tickets. "What're you doing in the next race?"

While they pore over their racing forms, betting odds, checking out trainers, how a horse does on mud, on grass, on ten furlongs, I make small bets based on how a horse holds its tail, what its number is, the confidence in a jockey's wave, but none of my horses come in. I splurge on the daily double, put it all on Time Flies to win. He doesn't, and I go home just slightly in the hole.

Twenty-nine

I am driving on the road from the Sierra Nevada toward Yosemite. I have been driving for five, maybe six hours, through one ghost town after another. Kate, in her car seat, has been fussing for a while. We stopped back in Victorville, at the Roy Rogers and Dale Evans Museum, where we gazed at Trigger, mounted, behind glass, in all his former splendor, and at Bullet. At the one hundred animals, now stuffed, that Roy killed with his own hands, his collection of wristwatches, the shrines to Roy and Dale's three dead children, no explanation given. Then we drove on.

I must be crazy, I tell myself, but still I keep going, farther and farther into the Mojave. We pause for late breakfast at the Olicante Ranchhouse. There are dead birds mounted everywhere, even on the tables, dead flies on the windowsills, Jesus pictures above the cash register, red curtains, several mooseheads, and German tourists. Taxidermists must do well in this neck of the woods. I order the cowboy breakfast, steak and eggs. Kate smears scrambled eggs into her mouth. After breakfast I clean her up and start to drive. We make it past Red Mountain, a boom town founded in 1837, now in ruins. Old cars line the dusty streets in junk heaps, gray laundry hangs on clothes lines.

When I got up that morning, I longed for home, for Manhattan and its gritty streets, for people in their frenzied pace. I couldn't take another weekend alone with no plans, no one to do anything with. No one I can count on. If we were in the city, I'd head to a museum, see a show. Walk around.

So once again I drive east on the Vegas road. Maybe I'll just keep driving all the way, but then I turn, thinking I'll make it to Yosemite and back in a weekend.

I drive by a house that is shingled outside in street signs, its parking lot filled with old tires and toy trucks, painted in primary colors. A sign reads: VISITORS WELCOME, so I stop.

Signs on the front of the house announce "Live Bombing Area," "Stop in the Name of Love," "Women Enter at Your Own Risk." It doesn't seem too inviting, but Kate is squirming, fidgeting. I could let her rest a little, maybe get a cold drink, assuming this is some kind of bar. A man comes out to greet us. "Please," he says. He wears a MAY THE FORCE BE WITH YOU T-shirt and introduces himself as Ted.

"What is this place?" I ask him, as I peer into the patio. It's covered by an old tarp supported by a red-and-white-striped barber pole.

"It's my house," he says, inviting us in. We sit in the patio, where giant coconuts and painted pine cones hang from a cactus. The patio is strung with Christmas lights, utility lights—"borrowed," Ted says, from the old railroad that used to run through here. He flips a switch and the Christmas lights come on, the railroad lights begin blinking on and off. Water starts to flow from overhead pipes into an open barrel of water, where plastic animals swim. Streamers made of flip tops, decorated with old eyelash curlers and pots and pans, including bedpans, dangle from the top of the tarp and are suddenly illumined in this strobe-light-and-water show.

Kate rearranges the plastic animals in the water, moves all kinds of pipes and wiring around, bangs Christmas ornaments together so they wave in the breeze, chases a litter of kittens, as I sip cold root beer. Ted brings me a plate of rice and beans, which tastes delicious. He says he's lived here for years now, on a pension. "I collect things," he tells me, as if I hadn't noticed. "I guess that's what drove my wife away."

We stay for an hour or so. I tell him I need to get back, and he offers us the guest room. He points skyward, and I see five narrow mattresses on the roof. "Up there?" I ask him.

I think how lovely it would be to sleep on his roof under the stars. Then I think that I don't know this man and that Kate could slip off the roof while I slept, so I decline.

"You know what you should call this place?" I say as we head to our car. "You should call it the Desert Mirage."

"I'll think about that," he says, pressing something into my hand. I glance down and see a nugget of solid gold.

Then Ted says, "Here, I got something for the kid." He hands her a small plastic statue of a friar. When he presses on the friar's head, his pants fall down and water squirts out of his penis. Ted starts to laugh and so does Kate, but I tuck the nugget into my pocket, grab Kate by the hand, and say to Ted, "I think we better get going."

Out in the parking lot, I can still hear him laughing.

Too tired to drive all the way back to Laguna, I stop at a Motel 6 near Barstow. We get a room for thirty-nine dollars and watch cartoons until we fall asleep. In the morning I drive straight to the beach, where Kate and I spend the day.

That night I am not home long when Jeremy calls. He says how much he misses us. That he's no good without us. He tells me that the woman who called on New Year's Eve is strange and obsessed. It won't happen again, he promises.

He says he wants to try again, so we make our Valentine's plans. If you come here, he says, we could plan something.

A Valentine's weekend back East. I think if I reserve early I can get a cheap flight.

"I love you," he tells me before he hangs up.

"Are you sure?" I ask. "Are you absolutely sure?"

"You are the sea in which I swim," he says.

Thirty

The astrologer Nostradamus (1503–66) has predicted that an enormous earthquake will end the world on May 10, 1988. One of the light workers who is part of a phone tree calls to inform me of this fact. Other Nostradamus predictions have come true. The verses "When the animal tamed by man/begins to speak after great effort and difficulty/the lightning so harmful to the rod/will be taken from the earth and suspended in the air" predicted radio.

Now, in the current revival of the 1982 documentary, *The Man Who Saw Tomorrow,* narrated by that prophet of doom Orson Welles, a Nostradamus quatrain predicts "a mighty trembling" in "the new city" on the day when all the planets will be aligned, which happens to be May 10, 1988. We should all be prepared, the worker tells me. It is possible that we'll be beamed up on that day. The planet, he tells me, is going to crumble.

"The time is upon us," he informs me. Special meetings will be called. Preparations are being made.

"Preparations for what?" I ask him.

"For the journey we are about to make to the next level," he says. He asks if I am ready, and I say I'm not sure.

"You need to be sure. All light workers must be sure of their missions."

He asks if I will continue the phone tree by calling five people. I agree and place my first call. A woman answers, and I tell her about Nostradamus and the world coming to an end May 10. She already knows. I call the second person on my list, and on the other end of the phone he starts to cry. "It's too early. It's too soon."

"It's okay," I tell him, feeling bad. "Maybe you've got more time."

A newspaper arrives in my mail, *Astrology and Psychic News,* published out of North Hollywood. I seem to be on various mailing lists now. I read the headlines: BLIND MAN RESCUES DROWNING DAUGHTER AT SEA. REJECTED LOVER ATTRIBUTES WITCH'S SPELL TO RETURN OF GIRLFRIEND. A woman lost 104 pounds with an Aztec-Mantax weight-loss amulet. A mother in Mexico City heard the screams of her little boy where he was trapped in an old refrigerator, ten miles away. Advertisements for healers and astrologers, palmists ("The future is in your hands") and psychics. The highly specialized psychics Angie talked to me about. The psychic of bad teeth, the psychic of unfinished tasks, the psychic of head injuries, the psychic of lost dogs.

A widower contacts a warlock to help him find an old girlfriend he lost touch with forty years before. But I read the rejected lover casting the witch's spell with the most interest. The lover hired a witch named Andreika to cast a spell. In his palm he saw his girlfriend's face; three weeks later she returned to him.

Reading this article, I stare into my palm, trying to conjure Jeremy's face. But he is nowhere to be seen.

The Dream Factory

Thirty-one

Igor Stravinsky once remarked: "The only way to avoid Hollywood is to live there." Thus far I have managed to avoid it, but now I no longer can. Sam Lauderstein—the poet who stood me up for lunch a few months ago—has invited me to a party in L.A. It is a benefit for a cause I believe in, and I'm told that Marsha Mason, the actress, will read a section of my new book, *Nothing to Declare.* I'm so excited I leave four hours early. The party is being held in a restaurant called Helene's, which has no sign (just look for the valet parking and the fancy people, I'm told), on a side street.

It's a good thing I allowed myself four hours, because it is rush hour and the 405 is jammed, and then I can't find the place. Finally I see the valet parking, the fancy people and cars. I arrive at nine, fashionably late, and enter the building through a side entrance with no sign.

The room is filled with very good cheekbones, toned bodies. I am in a white jumpsuit, but everyone else is in black. Someone stops me and says, "I love that jumpsuit. I'm going to start wearing white."

One wall seems to be a giant mirror. I can see the bar, the fire burning in the fireplace, the people sitting at the tables, all reflected there. Since I am feeling nervous, I decide to go over and check my makeup, comb my hair.

I walk up to the mirror, but when I look in it, I'm not there. There is no reflection of me at all.

Then I realize that it is not a mirror but a window, carved out of a wall, and that on the other side there is a bar, a fireplace, people dressed in black, just like in the room where I stand.

"You can take Hollywood for granted like I did, or you can dismiss it with the contempt we reserve for what we don't understand. It can be understood too, but only dimly and in flashes." Cecilia Brady, the narrator of F. Scott Fitzgerald's *The Last Tycoon*, says. Perhaps I'd been taking it for granted. Now I wanted to understand it. Water, weather, film, and freeways, that was how I understood the pull of this place.

The popular myth is that Thomas Edison invented the movies. This is only partly true. In fact, the film industry began with a bet by Leland Stanford, the railroad magnate, that a horse at a single gallop lifted all four feet off the ground. Stanford hired Eadweard Muybridge, the photographer, to prove he was right. Muybridge placed twelve cameras around a racetrack and shot the now-famous sequence of a horse at full gallop.

Edison took Muybridge's achievement a step further. Instead of using a series of cameras to record an event, Edison invented a single camera that could take a series of pictures. It was this stroke of genius that perhaps more than anything has shaped the history of Southern California. The first true sequence of film footage captured Edison's laboratory assistant, Fred Ott, in the act of sneezing. This image was shown inside a cabinet called a Kinetoscope and became one of the biggest attractions at the Chicago World's Fair in 1893.

It took a storyteller named Edwin S. Porter to take the concept of moviemaking out of the laboratory and into the music halls. Instead of filming an incident, Porter, who worked as a cameraman for the Edison Company, made one up. In 1903 *The Life of an American Fireman* told the story of the rescue of a woman and her child from a burning building. Next came America's first crime movie, *The Great Train Robbery.* These films were projected onto sheets hung in abandoned buildings, where thousands of people, willing to pay a nickle apiece, flocked to see them.

Edison knew a good thing when he saw it. In 1909 Edison created the Motion Picture Patents Company, whose purpose was to grant licenses to those who wanted to use the new technology. But others wanted to cash in. To flee the patent police, many would-be filmmakers headed west. In the hills of Los Angeles it was difficult to track down the violators, who could shoot and edit films in a matter of days. And, if all else failed, they could make it to Mexico in a day.

Los Angeles exists because of three elements: the filmmakers who pirated Thomas Edison's invention of the moving picture and took it as far west as they could get from the New York court orders to stop them; the inventions of the airplane and the automobile; and the discovery of a narrow vein of water, enough to irrigate a city. The dream factory is a postmodernist dream—a city on the fringe of history, without a real history of its own, beyond that of its own invention.

Sam Lauderstein, who organized this event, finds me, hovering in a corner near the bar. He informs me that the actor/director Griffin Dunne, who has just read from *Postcards from the Edge,* wants to meet me. On our way over, Sam introduces me to someone. "Mary, I want you to meet my great friend, the ex-star of the ex-series *Hill Street Blues."*

The guy gets up from his seat and says, "Actually it was *St. Elsewhere,"* but already Sam Lauderstein is pulling me along.

We find Griffin Dunne sitting at the other end of the bar, nursing a beer. He is a dark, thoughtful person, almost brooding,

I think, as he shakes my hand. He tells me he's got a copy of my last book in his briefcase (that's why he wanted to meet me), and he's going to take it with him to New York the next day.

"Hey, Griffin," a young man interrupts us. "It's been so long. What coast you working on these days?"

Griffin pats the young man on the arm. "The gold coast."

Then Griffin bends close to my ear. He starts talking to me about Baja and how you could just die there. The sky is so blue and the beach so white and the whales just follow the shore. He says that's the thing about travel—you go somewhere and say, I could just die right here and it would be fine.

A woman with blond hair pulled back in a ponytail gives Griffin a hug. "Darling, you were fabulous, just wonderful. Haven't seen you since *After Hours,* but you were really great."

Griffin gives her a wave, then turns back to me. "Anyway, where was I? Travel. I want to do a film about travel. My partner, she loved your last book. . . ."

"Hey, Griffin, remember me? The red-eye about two years ago, business class. We talked all night. . . ."

"Oh, sure, I remember. . . ."

"Mr. Dunne, excuse me, but will you be dining?" a waiter asks.

He says he will, then turns back to me. "So you're living in Laguna. I spent a night at the Ritz-Carlton. . . ."

"I had lunch there with my mother a few weeks ago."

"Well, then you know what I'm talking about. Nine hundred dollars a night. Can you imagine? A studio was paying for it, but nine hundred dollars."

"Could you see the ocean?"

"You'd better, for nine hundred a night."

Another person stops us, tugs at Griffin's arm. "You changed my life, Mr. Dunne. I want you to know that; you changed my life." Griffin gives him a pat on the arm, as if to say "Anytime."

"So, Mary," turning back to me. "Where were we?"

I don't remember, and neither does he, but he says he's going to read my book when he crosses the country. Then he gives someone the signal that he's coming to dinner, and I drive back to Laguna, imagining him reading my book on the red-eye and, as soon as his plane touches down in New York, making the offer that will change everything.

Thirty-two

A special meeting of light workers has been called to discuss Project Evacuation. We are asked to show up Sunday afternoon at the Laguna Hills home of Sharon and Randall, two members of the earth-based unit. The caller who leaves a message informs me that this is a very important meeting and involves our preparations for the destruction of the world scheduled for May 10, when the planets are aligned.

Since it is nearby and children are welcome (they are the next generation, after all, Wanda has said), I take Kate, driving the winding road to an address at Top of the World. There I'm greeted by two blond children with large heads, silent and morose. The little boy keeps shooting at the company with a laser gun. The girl is dressed, head to toe, in pink. The house is solar passive and ultra organized. Not a piece of paper is out of place. There's no sign of clutter. I wonder if anyone really lives here.

Five pairs of Dutch wooden shoes are lined up at the entranceway. Green carpeting is everywhere, and the walls are covered with mirrors. Dolls sit in chairs like babies. The goldfish bowl has a picture of life under the sea as a backdrop. The fish keep bumping their heads against it. The little boy with the laser gun shoots us if we reach for a cookie on the platter. After a while no one eats.

I notice Kate clomping around in a pair of wooden shoes. Sharon gives her a scolding look and tells the little boy with the laser gun to take Kate into the playroom. To her credit, Kate howls and refuses, then settles down at my feet. The little boy straightens up the wooden shoes, under his mother's scrutiny, before he disappears down the hall.

There are seven or eight of us, smiling believers. One young man has recently been visited, and tells us that from time to time, like when he's at the pool, he hears a swishing of their ships going by. "All of a sudden," he says, "I'll hear that sound." Of course, they are invisible, but he knows they're there. Wanda sits in the center of the couch in her pink jumpsuit, her flying-saucer earrings, a giant crystal around her neck, white leather boots, looking ready for departure.

She informs us that today we will receive a counseling talk about Project Evacuation. Armageddon, as we know, is imminent. It is possible that on May 10, as Nostradamus predicted, the earth will be destroyed. "But," she assures us, "we have nothing to worry about. In fact, this is a good sign. It is the realignment of the solar system." The ETs have us on their computers and "mailing lists." They know who their light workers are, and they are preparing to beam us up. We are their earth-bound angels. We will be saved in the face of any cataclysm ahead.

Nine new planets that resemble earth are being prepared, Wanda tells us. They are being equipped with trees and animals and fruit and all the bountiful things. "We have been studied for a long time and now are being offered a new paradise. What you need to understand about extraterrestrials is that earth is like their national park. Our planet is their Yosemite, their Yellowstone. We are their endangered species. They have come to protect us, to save us. The planets they are preparing will have no technology, no waste or pollution. Since there are nine of them, there will be no overcrowding. The climate will be perfect. It will be like heaven." There are contented nods and smiles all around.

Those of us who are not ready for the fourth dimension can have a little more time in the third. A special limbo-like planet is being prepared for that purpose. But once we are ready, we will leave our vessels behind (and with this she points to our bodies), we will leave them behind on the earthly plane and be beamed to the etheric plane, where the new planets await us. We'll be the first aboard, Wanda informs us. We have been chosen to lead the way. No mission has ever been as great as this. We just have to do Ashtar's work on the planet earth. We are the seeders of the great light worker movement, we are the souls that will be saved when this temporal planet comes to an end, we will ascend to the starships. We will know when they are coming; already there have been signs.

They came fifty years ago, but we were not ready to accept them. The government captured some and did experiments on them. So they have waited until the earth workers are ready, until we are prepared. Their starships will come with a great cataclysm. An earthquake will shatter the planet; a great comet will head this way. A war will threaten our destruction. But now the light workers are trained. We know what to expect.

In the hallway, the little boy makes his way, laser gun raised, ready to shoot us again.

Thirty-three

Shake, Rattle, and Roll meets in a small gymnasium not far from the house, and I take Kate to a class one Saturday morning. When I arrive, a dozen or so toddlers are on the floor. Their mothers sit around a giant blue and yellow and red (primary colors) parachute, each holding a corner. As the instructor puts on a tape of "Shake, Rattle, and Roll" and "She Loves You, Yah, Yah, Yah," the mothers lift the parachute and the toddlers crawl, teeter, or run under it.

Kate decides to head in the opposite direction, and she crawls to the side where another mother is standing. Alice introduces herself. She is Australian and, like Kate, her daughter is soon to be a year old. This is the third Shake, Rattle, and Roll class Alice has attended. "It's pretty appalling around here, isn't it?" Alice says.

Afterward we take our daughters out for ice cream and then down to the sandbox. The girls play, sharing toys. We spend the afternoon together and make a lunch date for later in the week.

After our second lunch date, Alice tells me something about her husband, Eric. Eric is very smart, as is Alice. I tell Alice about my work, about attending meetings where Ashtar speaks, and Alice says, "Oh, I know all about that. Eric has been visited."

"Visited?" I ask.

"Yes, by little people. That's how he describes them. They come to him in his dreams, early in the morning. Little bald people with almond-shaped eyes. They prod him, he says. He has a friend who had the same dream about them. He sees little people from time to time. Not recently, not anymore, but he has."

"What, exactly, do they look like?"

We are walking past a bookstore, and Alice points to a copy of *Communion*, by Whitley Strieber, in the window. "They look like that," she says.

In an interview in *The New York Times Book Review*, William Goyen, a novelist I admire, is asked if it isn't true that his characters are either waiting for something or wounded. And Goyen replies: "I think they are waiting for miracles, for wonderful visitations. . . . They're probably waiting for the marvelous . . . for the wonderful surprise. It's probably waiting for the Second Coming, underneath. I'm sure that's all I've ever been writing about. Salvation, redemption, freedom from bondage, complete release. All those people from all those little towns, that's what they were brought up to wait for: the end of the world, when the trumpets would sound and they'd be free of all this daily labor."

The first thing I notice about the goddess is her feet. The way they overlap oddly, one toe resting on the next. The fourth toe seems to rise from the middle of her foot. I glance over at Alice, who has brought me here. Her eyes are fixed on the feet as well. She gives me an odd wave. We have been instructed to leave our shoes and our intellect at the door. That is why I am able to stare at the feet of Fay, or Divine Mother of Earth, as she is "affectionately" called. The Laguna bungalow we've been invited to is decorated entirely with hearts—heart doormat, signs over the door, soap, dishes, notepads, pillows, candles. Even "Please take off your shoes" appears in a heart. Heart-shaped cookies are served on a heart-shaped tray.

We have been invited to participate in a totally intuitive experience, to reach into our tendermost parts and draw from our female nature. The goddess has come from the Midwest to offer a workshop on the divinity of women. "Our purpose," she tells us, "is to find upliftment in unconditional love."

As we sit in a circle, Divine Mother informs us that her workshop, which costs just $150, promises to "empower your feminine nature, heal negative emotions, attract your perfect mate and what you desire, learn to communicate, and experience the source of your female nature and where your divinity lies."

The mauve brochure has a picture of a woman sitting on a bed, putting up her hair. Divine Mother's symbol is a heart with a pyramid through it.

We sit mute, listening for about an hour as Divine Mother tries to sign us up. She wants women to really get in touch with their feminine side and in doing so get in touch with her power. The feminine is powerful; we just haven't learned to utilize it, that's all. The goddess offers us a total opening of the heart if we will just open our pocketbooks.

Afterward Alice and I go out for a beer. "It's a little like bringing coals to Newcastle, isn't it?" Alice says in her thickest Australian accent. I nod, sipping my beer. "Mary, why are you doing this?"

I shake my head. I think of William Goyen's statement about his characters, all either wounded or waiting. At first I thought my interest here was prurient, idle curiosity. Now I wonder if I'm not waiting for a miracle too. Some sign that I can turn my life around. "I don't really know," I tell her. "I'm really not sure." And I'm not.

It is Kate's first birthday, and I have a party. I invite Alice and her daughter, Robin, and Patricia and her son, Jake. Ramona picks up a piñata in Santa Ana and brings a few of her friends along. I buy an ice cream cake, which the children dive into. They run around outside, chasing a cat. I keep thinking a present will arrive, a card, something from Jeremy. Then it does come—a dozen roses.

I know I should be happy with this, but somehow it seems strange. When I talk to him later, I ask him if he couldn't have gone out and gotten her a gift. "What's she going to do with roses? Why not get her something so she'll think of you?"

"I wasn't sure what she'd like," he says.

"Like? She's a baby. She likes stuffed animals, toys, whatever."

"Next time I'll send her a toy."

Thirty-four

A few weeks later Jeremy calls to cancel our Valentine's plans. Not to cancel them, exactly, but to alter them in such a way that it is practically impossible for me to come to see him. He pleads his long, convoluted case—perhaps the one skill that applies to both his life and his legal involvements. He forgot that he had promised to take his boys skiing up at Stowe that weekend, and would I mind flying with Kate to Burlington instead of New York. He knows it will mean taking three planes and realizes this is inconvenient. When I mention that it will also be expensive, he balks. "You know I can't help you out, not now anyway."

"How will I ski with the baby?"

"Well, we could take turns watching her."

I decline. I have already had the experience of his watching her. "You don't really want to see me, do you? You don't really want me to come."

"Of course I want you to come. How can you say that?"

"I don't know," I shout into the phone. "I just can." I slam the receiver down.

I am five or six years old, and my father tells me that we are going somewhere. Somewhere I don't want to go, but he describes the place for me. He says it's a house in an orchard with apple and peach and plum trees; I can pick fruit just by reaching up my hand. He tells me that in the back of the house there is a river, where fish swim. I am convinced, and we drive and drive. It is a long way, and the road is dull and flat.

We arrive at a little house in a dark woods, and I race out back, to find three or four small, barren trees, a creek trickling through. No matter how long I search, I cannot find any fruit. I stand for hours tossing rocks into the stream, and no one can prod me away.

This is the first lie I recall being told, not a malicious lie, but a lie nonetheless. One intended to get me to do something I would not have done otherwise. I cannot call it a familiar feeling, but it is one I'll remember from time to time.

• • •

Was it two years ago? Or more? I can no longer recollect. They have blurred into one. A woman was visiting Jeremy. A colleague from somewhere—India, Norway. It doesn't matter. It was another weekend when he could not see me. When he was busy with important meetings. Saving the world. Who was I to argue with that? There was a case in The Hague. A group of Kurds were sitting in the living room, teacups on their laps, asking him to speak in their behalf.

Jeremy told me that maybe, maybe Sunday night he'd be free. I knew I shouldn't have, but I waited for him. I avoided friends and spent all day Saturday getting my work out of the way. On Sunday morning I cleaned my apartment, took a walk, though I didn't want to be out for long. I didn't want to miss his call. If I missed his call, it might just be that moment when he could come over, when he was at Grand Central. Sunday afternoon I phoned him and kept getting his machine. I left messages, one after the other. Perhaps he was in the city. Perhaps he was in Rome.

Should I wait for him to call, or go to a movie alone? Maybe I could still meet a friend, a friend who hadn't grown weary of listening to me complain (there weren't many of them left), go out to dinner. Act like a normal person. But most friends would shake their heads now when I told them how when I was with Jeremy, though it wasn't very often, I was as happy as could be. How we were soul mates. How this was meant to be. Friends, if they had known me a long time, didn't get it, but they tried.

Sunday evening came and went. I watched the clock as it got later, then I went out for cigarettes. When I came back my message light was blinking. Jeremy said he was calling from Penn Station. He had been out all day with whoever was visiting. "Why aren't you ever there when I need you?" he said. "Where do you go? If you were there, I'd be over." His message went on and on about how it's a shame we can never get together, how much he missed me.

I began to drink some vodka. I'd planned to have only a sip, maybe with Jeremy, but now I put lots of ice into a tall glass, squeezed in a lot of lime. Then I sat there, smoking and drinking. And leaving messages on Jeremy's machine. I called him names. A liar, a cheat.

I thought of my father telling me we were going to a house with an orchard and a river. I knew now that that was nothing. A white lie you tell a child, hardly a fib. No malice intended. But this was out of my league. F. Scott Fitzgerald was right. The East is filled with distortion; the Midwest never really told me a lie. I don't know how long I drank, but when Jeremy phoned from home, he was very disturbed. He said I don't trust. I take things too literally. Of course he wanted to be there for me. It was just a matter of time. The words sounded good. He was improvising, but it's what he was very good at.

I listened for a long time. He was still talking when I got a funky sleeping bag down from the closet, curled into it with another glass of vodka. He was still talking when I fell asleep. In the morning the phone was beeping, off the hook. My head was reeling, and I phoned my friend Michael and told him I spent the night on my floor with a bottle of vodka and that I thought I was going to kill myself.

Michael said, "How do you take your coffee, and what kind of bagel do you want?"

"Milk, no sugar, sesame," I muttered, and before I knew it, Michael was at my door, breakfast in hand. He fed me juice, aspirin. "What are you doing to yourself?" he asked me.

"I don't know. I love him."

Michael shook his head. "You love what you can't have," he told me, and, of course, this was true. But it didn't stop me.

I spent the next weekend with Jeremy. We took long walks in the woods, we read the paper. We were a couple again. On Sunday he went to play tennis, and he was gone for a very long time. All morning. Then there was a football game to watch. We fought about this. We fought about how there was never any time. We fought about the weekend before.

"Who is it?" I shouted at him. "Who are you seeing?"

We were arguing in the bedroom when I grabbed the scissors. Not sure of what I intended to do with it, I held it up. Then I stabbed the bed—a bed I had come to despise—ten, fifteen times. Jeremy stood back, watching me. As I was stabbing, I thought to myself: I don't know this person. I didn't mean him. I meant me.

Jeremy was invited to China. He asked me if I wanted to go. My way would be paid. He wanted me along. Come with me, please, he said, I don't want to go alone. It didn't take much convincing. I looked at maps and saw that we could travel on from Beijing and go to Russia via Siberia, a trip I'd always wanted to take, but Jeremy booked a lecture tour to New Zealand a week after we were due back from China.

"Can't New Zealand wait?" I asked, but Jeremy said no.

"We will have three weeks. Isn't that enough?" But, of course, it was not enough. It would never be enough. I was addicted as surely as if this relationship were a drug, were booze.

Together we wandered the streets of Beijing. We sampled delicacies (sea cucumbers that slithered down the throat, sesame chicken feet), and we laughed at our guide, Chen, who held up his watch and declared us always late. We escaped Chen and rented bicycles and rode around Beijing, eating dumplings in a corner shop. On a boat down the Yangtze we made love in our little cabin. It was a hot, desultory day. Dead pigs and a few bloated human bodies drifted by. We sailed through the gorges that were soon to be flooded for a dam, and there, as we made love, a sharp pain coursed through my body, like nothing I had felt before.

During my pregnancy, Jeremy traveled all the time. When he was not traveling, he was under tremendous pressure. It is true, there were many demands on him. Many sudden demands. I was seven months pregnant, and I had my bicycle on campus. This was how I got around. One afternoon it rained and the temperature dropped. The weather turned icy, a chilling cold. The sidewalks and paths were glazed in ice.

I called Jeremy in his office and asked if he was going into the city. He said he was, and I asked for a lift.

What time? he said, hemming and hawing. Then he told me Sigrid was in town from Denmark. They had a meeting to attend.

"Wasn't that the woman who called once at four A.M.?" But Jeremy didn't remember those late-night phone calls from the Danish woman.

"Well, anyway, she's here."

"So I'll ride with you."

But there were problems. He wasn't sure of the time. He wasn't sure of what train. There might be delays. I'd better go ahead.

It was dark when I set out, walking my bicycle across campus to the train. The ground was slippery, and I almost fell several times. I had to be very careful walking, because of the sheer ice. Where there was snow, the ground was particularly dangerous. You couldn't see how treacherous it was.

Natural Disasters

Thirty-five

At a reading at Fahrenheit 451, our neighborhood bookstore in Laguna, I meet Willa. She is sipping wine and has read my work. She is also from Illinois, a town near mine, and is named after Willa Cather, my favorite Midwestern writer. Willa is a writer herself, with a good sense of humor, a head of thick reddish hair, and, I will soon discover, a good backhand. I tell her I am interested in local lore, and she says, "Oh, I can give you a lot of that."

We leave the bookstore, and over drinks she starts to tell me about the Saint Ann's woman. The Saint Ann's woman is a fourteen-thousand-year-old skeleton found in an excavation on Saint Ann's Street. It turned out to have been placed there as an archaeological scam to "prove" that people were in the area prior to when migration theory said they were.

She tells me about Arthur, a local archaeologist who gets assigned to all foundation excavations in California—in accordance with California law—in case Indian remains are found. He came to her house once and stood against her fireplace, his erection bulging out of his brown polyester pants, and said she could read his paper on the Saint Ann's woman if he could have his way with her.

We are laughing at this when Willa points to a woman across the room and tells me that her specialty is having racially mixed children. She has a Tahitian child, a Hispanic, a black, and a Scandinavian. The fathers have nothing to do with the kids. Their upkeep is paid for by her incredibly rich alcoholic grandmother, who made her millions by buying Laguna property cheap in the 1960s, when nobody wanted to live here because of the drug and hippie culture. The grandmother is a terribly prejudiced person, and though she supports them, she doesn't particularly like the kids. The mother is on lithium and now seems to want a Chinese baby. Their Christmas card looks like it was issued by UNICEF.

Willa walks me home. She first offers me a ride in her car, but it is a beautiful night and the bougainvillea is in bloom, and I tell her I prefer to walk. It is out of her way, but she doesn't seem to mind. In fact, Willa does not seem to be in a hurry to be anywhere. It is what I'll come to really like about her.

We climb the hill and I tell her about Kate, how I'm out here on my own. "Her father isn't quite in the picture," I say, confessing to Willa what I've had trouble confessing to myself. The wind blows bougainvillea blossoms our way as she tells me about her daughter, her ex, and her boyfriend, Jimmy, who lives in Malibu. "You'll have to come up one weekend," she says. "His house sits on the median tide line of the Pacific Ocean."

"How does it do that?"

"You'll see."

Last year Jimmy had to have his groins removed. At great cost. He also had to have some of his pilings replaced. This is explained to me as Willa drives along the Pacific Coast Highway toward his house, which sits on a wedge of beach between the rocky cliffs of Malibu and the ocean. "Groins?" I ask.

These are structures that jut out from beneath houses and are supposed to keep the sand from receding, but they don't work. Ladders that extend down to the beach are now two or three feet off the ground. The lawyer who lives a few doors down fell off his ladder a few months ago and broke his leg. "That's why we're being sued," Willa explains.

"Sued?"

"Because we had the groins removed. Oh, we're friends with the lawyer, but he's still suing us."

We pull up in front of a bungalow that has a mountain at its back, the ocean in front of it. When we walk in, we have to shield our eyes. The living room is all light and water, with flowers in a bowl. The bedroom is a picture window of the Pacific Ocean. With all this spareness and light, I feel as if I have walked into a Hockney. I have to put on my sunglasses to sit inside the house.

Beneath the house, waves crash, rocks are thrown up against the pilings so that it sounds "as if you're in a bowling alley," Jimmy says. "The median tide line," Jimmy informs me, "is right about where you're sitting."

He's a relaxed man in his early fifties, dressed in jeans and a polo shirt. This breezy living seems to suit him, though it is precarious. The house is all white and wood and I tell him that it looks as if one strong wind, wave, or mud slide would take it out to sea. "Well," Jimmy says, handing me a glass of Chianti, "it would."

Kate frolics on the deck with Harlequin, the cat, and stares out as a pair of dolphins leap in the surf just outside the bedroom. From Jimmy's deck there is an unobstructed vista, an endless horizon. I want to show all of this to Jeremy. I want him to see what I see. The ocean glistens, and suddenly I don't blame anyone for wanting to live here. Suddenly I see it all—all of what California holds. Eureka. For a moment I want to live here too.

But it is not without its costs. "Last year we had to be evacuated when the fires jumped the highway," Jimmy says, putting his legs up on the railing of his deck. "One bad storm could wipe us out. Our neighbor, he was washed out with a mud slide in 1982 during El Niño. That's why I keep these big boots on the deck." He points to knee-high blue vinyl boots. "And that ladder, so we can climb on the roof if the mountain slides down. My neighbor got the worst case of poison oak. The mud that came down from the mountains was soaked with it. That mud almost hit my house, but at the last moment it turned and went into his. He just opened his front door and let it go through." Jimmy taps on the wall that divides his neighbor's house from his. "The problem with mud is it's unpredictable. It's not like rain. Mud unsettles the mountain. It can build slowly. You can't imagine what it's like when a twelve-foot-high wall of mud comes sliding down the road. And it can come on a sunny day weeks after a storm. I'm insured for mud within forty-eight hours of a storm, but not after that." Jimmy runs his hand through his hair, shakes his head. "And it can come at any time."

"My God," I say, gazing up at the hills and out to sea. "How can you live like that?"

"Look at this," Jimmy says, pointing at his unobstructed view. Outside of Alaska, California has more coastline than any other state in the United States. "It's worth whatever sacrifices we have to make." I gaze at the dolphins, at the shimmering sea, and think he is probably right.

Willa laughs, shrugs. "Tell her about your brother."

"Oh, my brother got a lot of money from the state because a mud slide wiped his house out in '82, and he put it into an apartment complex in Van Nuys, but an earthquake wiped out the apartment and he lost it because he missed a premium payment. Well, that was just bad luck. You know, we love it here."

Willa nods in assent. "All my life," she says, "I've been safe. I like that I'm not safe here."

Jimmy waves at us, and we follow him through the open living room toward the front of his house, which abuts the Pacific Coast Highway. To the side of the house is a hatch, which he lifts open, and there is the ocean. I take Kate's hand and we follow him below and it is as if we are under a ship. All around us are rows and rows of concrete and wood pilings, holding up the houses that line this Malibu coast, some of which have already been abandoned due to damage. "I love this. I love the fact that the sea is right at my steps. That the tide line is under my living room." Peering down, we see that it is. Just at the base of his steps is the beach, the waves striking the supports of his house. "But I've got this idea," he says, leading us back up to the deck. "I'm going to build a big trapdoor, and when it rains, I'll open the trap. Maybe I'll put a grate over it so that nobody falls through, and then when the mud comes it will go down the trap and out to sea instead of into my living room."

We stand staring at where the trapdoor would go. Through the slates of the deck, I can see the ocean, pounding the shore. That night I sleep in bed with Kate to the sound of waves under the house, rocks banging beneath our room like bowling pins.

Thirty-six

Isadore "Irish" Figler is an old Chicago boy who works the Big Wheel at the Riviera in Vegas. He's a friend of some friends of my mother, who has told me that if I make it back to Vegas, "Irish" will show me around. Irish Figler? I ask her, but she says that's his name. And don't call him, she tells me. Just show up.

I make a weekend arrangement with Ramona, agreeing to pay her overtime (surely I'll make up the money in Vegas). I leave at the crack of dawn, heading due east from my house, past Barstow, past Summit—a desert road I've come to know fairly well. I stop for gas. I eat a decent breakfast, and by lunchtime I'm checking into the Nugget, which is cheaper than the big hotels on the Strip. In the lobby I find myself surrounded by slots and by old ladies who wear gloves to keep their hands from bleeding.

I head over to the Riviera, where it doesn't take too long to find a nice Jewish "boy" with flaming red hair and pale-green eyes, built like prime rib, with a silver dollar set inside a gold ring on one of many chains dangling around his hairy neck. He sees me skulking up to the wheel he spins. When I tell him I'm the girl from Chicago Ira sent, Irish gives his wheel one last spin. Then he shouts to his pit boss, "I'm on break. I gotta take this dame around." His boss, a balding man in a black tuxedo, gives him a shrug.

We head over to the bar, where we order Diet Cokes. When he's sure he's out of earshot of his pit boss, he points a finger in my face. "Never, never bet on the wheel. You can bet on blackjack," Irish tells me. "You've got your best chance there, especially if you're a systems player, but the rest of the stuff is a crap shoot, literally. You may as well be playing Russian roulette." We sit down at a table in a quiet corner of the casino. "I been in this town years now, don't ask me how many. I can tell you there's more people buried in the hills than in the cemeteries. Anyway, in Vegas, if you ain't got money, you got memories."

After our Cokes, Irish tells his pit boss he's gone for the day. The boss gives another shrug, as if this doesn't surprise him, and tells him to have a good time. I figure that since my mother set up this meeting it's safe, but still it's a little strange to be moving through the world of Vegas with a dealer I just met. He takes me over to Vegas World, where I stare up at the starry ceiling, the giant purple illuminated pods, lava lamps everywhere, a weightless astronaut sailing overhead. A giant wheel-of-fortune space station.

"You got some money?" Irish asks me. I tell him I have a little. I've brought two hundred for gambling. The rest for a night in a hotel, a visit to a spa in the morning, and the drive home. "Okay. Let's get you some chips." He gets me two hundred dollars' worth of white, red, green, and black chips. "You need five hundred bucks for a blue one; you ain't got five hundred, do you?"

I shake my head. "That's okay," he says. "Let's see if you can't win us dinner." On our way to blackjack, Irish pauses at a poker table. He scrutinizes the game there, then pulls me away. "See that guy?" He points to a nerdy-looking young man in glasses, a suit—a loser if I ever saw one. "He's a sitting bull, a pro. He pretends he doesn't know how to play, then he beats your pants off. Let's get outta here."

He tugs me off to the blackjack tables and finds a game and a dealer he likes. "Okay," Irish says. "Hit me." The dealer begins to deal. I'm just sitting there, but I watch Irish tell the dealer when to hit him, when to raise him. If there is a system here, it's lost on me, but Irish seems to know it. He wins a little for me, then loses a little. I whisper into his ear, "Let's do something else," pointing to roulette. He shakes his head. "Never the wheel, never the slots."

An hour later he's made me a hundred dollars. "Okay, cash in your chips. Let's take a ride. I'll show you where people live."

But I want to keep playing. He earned me an easy hundred. That should take care of dinner. Now maybe he could earn me a few hundred more to cover Ramona's weekend cost. "Let's play some more."

He shakes his head, walking through the windowless, clockless casino. "Nope."

• • •

His car is silver and smells a little oily. The passenger seat is pushed far back and I can't move it up, but I'm enjoying Irish's company. We drive along, and he points out the sights. "That's where the Mirage is going up after they tear the Flamingo down."

I tell Irish I want to stop and gamble some more.

"You've played enough," he says. "We won a little. That's good. That's enough. The compulsive gambler, he's really playing to lose. If you don't quit when you're ahead, then you're a loser, pretty simple. Throw caution to the wind, that's the sign of a loser. They want money to cover everything, like a blanket over your real self."

Realizing that I've got some version of the Vegas Prophet with me, I just let Irish drive me down Paradise Road toward the west side of town. We pass the Guardian Angels Catholic Church near the Desert Inn, pass the Wee O'Kirt of the Heather marriage chapel, in the direction of what Irish calls the Naked City. That's a trailer park where showgirls used to live. It was called the Naked City because the girls sunbathed nude to get even tans.

He points to a fence, and on the other side I imagine those showgirls, their bodies bronzed, naked, men like Irish peering over the fence. "In this town," Irish goes on apropos of nothing, "you're living in hope and you're dying in spirit. You gotta gamble. If, if, if . . . when, when, when . . . Like a junkie. A gambler will do anything, just so he can play one more day. If he can't play, he gets depressed. He'll steal. I know women, nice women, who sell their bodies. . . ."

As he drives, I can't help thinking that I've got a hundred dollars more than I came with and if we could just keep on at blackjack, then maybe I'd really get ahead.

We pull into a trailer park, where an old woman with

bleached hair and lipstick riding up the creases above her lips is standing on her AstroTurf porch. "Irish," she shouts. "Come on in and have a beer."

When we get out, I take a closer look at Selma. A ton of blue makeup is smeared around her eyes, and Selma has no hair, actually, mainly scabs and a very bad wig. She has plastic flowers in pots all around her trailer, and there are Christmas ornaments on the trees. She seems very happy to see us.

In a matter of minutes Selma tells me how she's from Minnesota and came here in the 1960s. She was a keno runner at Bally's. "Never left," she tells me. She also never married, though she lives with her boyfriend, Al, who's a bellman at the Tropicana and, she tells me with a cackle, awaiting the Messiah.

That night over dinner, Irish informs me that the first sign of insanity in Vegas is to lose and keep laughing. The I-don't-care attitude. "You know," he goes on, looking into his Scotch, "success can be counted in lots of ways, not just money, but in this town the bottom line is money. Nothing else matters. Not the good deeds you do or the cures for cancer you find or the beautiful poems you write. Just money matters. You can't buy love, let me tell you. I've comped my nieces and nephews and friends so many times, but that doesn't buy me love." Irish looks sad now; maybe he knows that I'm just one more person he's never going to see again. "But still I like to sit around and tell stories and lie."

When the check comes, Irish picks up the tab despite my protests. "But you won me that hundred."

"That's okay, lady, go home rich." He asks me to kiss his silver-dollar ring. "And get lucky," he says.

Thirty-seven

At first light I drive straight back through the Mojave. The desert shimmers in morning light—golden, rose, and purple hues. All the way back I am thinking. I cannot stop thinking. About the risks I've been taking lately. About Kate. When I am away from her—a night here, a night there—I miss her milky breath, the sweat on her curls. There is this restlessness in me, as if I can't stop. I can't sit still. Nothing makes me feel right. The questions I can't answer seem to loom. Why did Jeremy break our Valentine's plans? Who called New Year's Eve? I am overlooking something. I don't see things quite right.

Arriving home just before noon, I realize I'm starting to get to know this road quite well. Too well. The road has given me a lot of time to think. That afternoon I phone Jeremy.

"That woman who called my house on New Year's—it was Sigrid, wasn't it?"

"Mary, aren't you tired of this?" Jeremy says with a sigh.

"Tell me. I want to know. Then I can decide for myself."

Jeremy says no, that woman didn't have an accent. She was just whispering into the phone.

"She had an accent. Was it Sigrid?" I ask.

"You don't know the person who called," he says.

"Is that why you broke our Valentine's plans? Because of her?"

"I broke them because of the boys. Now, Mary, you're being silly. This isn't the way to act." He is being parental with me, authoritative. He sounds firm, sure of himself. I can see him arguing his case in a court of law. I want to believe him. I want to believe every word he says, but I don't.

I throw a fit. I think I am right, but he keeps telling me I'm wrong. The film *Gaslight* comes to mind. I feel as if I am being driven mad. "Tell me the truth," I shout at him. "Just tell me the truth, once and for all. I have a child. A child with you. I have a right to know."

It occurs to me as I say this that nowhere is it written that he is her father. He never signed the affidavit required to have his name on her birth certificate. This has been a source of much anger between us. He said you get the papers and I said you get the papers, and in the end no one got the papers and he never signed them. Perhaps I never wanted him to. "I have a child," I tell him again, "and I am responsible for her."

"I'm telling you the truth." His voice grows impatient, yet he never yells. Never screams. He is so gentle and assured, so convincing. So why don't I believe him? What is wrong with me that everything feels like a lie?

I hang up on him, and for the next several nights I bite my knuckles so as not to phone him. Let him come to me. I try to force myself not to wait for him to call me at night. But I break down: A day can't go by when I don't speak with him. If I don't hear from him by bedtime, I leave long messages on his machine.

I know how to give up an addiction. I've done it before. You break the cycle. I did it with cigarettes. So why can't I do it now?

Angie senses that something is wrong. She takes one look at me and wrinkles her brow. When I lie down, she puts smooth purplish stones in my hands, on my sternum, on my forehead. "This is imperial jasper," Angie tells me as she lays on the cool stones. "They are for someone who is unfocused, who wants to get focused. Imperial jasper is for a high-female-energized person who wants to get grounded."

For the first time the stones seem to vibrate across my brow. Their coolness makes my eyes relax, grow weary. Then she digs into her drawer and finds something else—a translucent green rock that appears to shimmer in her hand. "What's that?" I ask, struck by the green glow. She places it gently in the middle of my forehead, and immediately a strange warmth emanates from it. "This is *agni mani*, the celestial gem," Angie tells me. "These are meteorites that come from outer space. The Sanskrit name translates to 'fire pearl.' "

When I close my eyes, I see a bright light. It seems to be shining out from the inside, and it feels warm. "Angie," I say, "what *is* that?" Soon my whole body feels warm, all the way to the extremities, but the warmth seems to be coming from within me.

She doesn't have to ask me what "that" refers to. "It's your Third Eye Chakra opening up," Angie says, squeezing my hand. "You're starting to see clearly again."

Ramona moves indifferently through all her tasks, except for taking care of Kate. When I am at work, she bathes and powders and fluffs her, puts ribbons in her hair, dresses her in her best outfits just to go to the store. I am slightly jealous of the attention she is able to give my child, jealous that I cannot stay home and wash her hair, comb out her curls, put her in little dresses. Envious that I have to work so hard. Even at night I have all these papers to grade, things to read, lessons to prepare. I seem never to have time just to be.

Still, I cannot help but notice that when Ramona is not fussing over Kate she looks miserable, like someone who is sick all the time. One day I take her aside. "Ramona, it's time. Go get your son."

Her face lights up. "But I don't know. The money . . ."

"We'll make do. Take a week, go get him."

"He won't eat much."

"Ramona, I'm not worried about how much he eats. Just tell your mother when you're coming." Ramona makes her plan to leave for Mexico.

She is gone a week, and I think I'll never see her again. While she is gone, Kate takes her first step. Though she's been toddling for a while, she's always held on to something; she didn't exactly walk. Now she does. I am sitting on the sofa, and Kate is holding my index fingers in her fists. Then she lets go and takes one step away from me, then another. "Oh, you surprised me," I tell her. "You've been working on that."

She is thirteen months old to the day, and she didn't try to walk until she could. As soon as she has learned to walk, she never falls down, except once. And then she pretends to be picking up a piece of thread. She is very careful, I tell myself, and she is very proud. It's bred in the bone. I believe this is a good sign.

For that week Kate spends the day at Monica's with Jenelle while I am at work. Then suddenly Ramona reappears. She has with her a beautiful boy with black hair and olive skin. Ramona is happy again, laughing when she does her tasks. Andreas sits in the living room with Kate, sharing picture books with her.

Jimmy and Willa invite me to see a play with some friends of theirs, and we meet at the Galaxy café, which Jimmy thinks will be right up my alley. It's true I love the flying-saucer fixtures. There are zap squiggles along the wall and pictures of "the stars"—Bianca Jagger, Liz Taylor, Marilyn Monroe. I order from the "Chicken of the Future" specials: Constellation Chicken served charbroiled on a bed of brown rice with cilantro. Willa orders the Halley's Comet omelette, with spinach, bacon, and jack cheese. Her friend Chris orders the Super Nova, which for some reason has shrimp, not nova, in it. Chris's wife, Joy, says she'll have some of ours.

Chris starts telling us stories about his brother, Lou. When Lou was sixteen, he was smoking a joint on top of a telephone pole with a friend. Lou toppled off the pole, landed on the high-voltage wire, got zapped with twelve thousand volts of electricity. All his jewelry got welded to his body. His friend managed to kick him off the power line.

Somehow Lou lived. He was in the hospital for four months. En route to visit him, Chris got into a motorcycle accident and wound up in the same hospital, a few rooms down. Lou had a roommate named Matt, who had tried to commit suicide after two open-heart surgeries, because he assumed he wasn't going to live anyway. After they all got out of the hospital, they took a trip around America for a year.

These are all survivors, Chris says. This is a story about survivors. I nod my head. I'm interested in survivors too. Lou is twenty-nine now. He got a forty-three-year-old flight attendant pregnant in a bathroom at the airport one night. A literal layover, Chris calls it. Last week—it seems this is why Chris is telling the story—Lou and the flight attendant got married in a hot-air balloon. "You shoulda seen them. Drifting across the Pacific, taking their vows." And I think I almost *can* see them.

The play was terrible. I don't remember much about it, but it was terrible. Afterward, however, we meet the theater's security guard. The Avantguardian, as he calls himself, has turned an old gas station into a place called Another Planet. He sings with a rock band called the Cosmic Kitten. He tells us that he comes from the constellation UMA, where the Umights and the Umightnots live.

The Avantguardian runs this novelty store out of his gas station, and he tells me about a book he likes called *Uranchia,* which is all about the government of heaven. He has also read the Air Force Blue Book on UFOs. "It's all a conspiracy," he says, but he won't say of what or by whom. "They're all out to get us." As we are leaving, he honks his horns, clangs his cymbals together.

He shouts his farewell as we disappear down the alleyway he guards. "Umight see me again, and then again Umightnot."

Thirty-eight

On Valentine's Day, Jeremy sends me a dozen red roses—the same kind he sent Kate on her birthday. He phones and sends cards. He is trying to get back into my good graces, and when at last I pick up the phone, his voice is sheepish, apologetic. "You don't know how complicated my life is," he tells me.

"Yes, I do, because you've made mine just as complicated."

"You don't have the demands on you that I have on me. All the papers I have to read, the work, the kids . . ."

Shifting the phone so I can cradle Kate, I gaze into my office, and the desk looks pretty full to me. I am a writer with a career, a teaching job, a book coming out (that will be surprisingly successful), another one in the drawer (that I will sell before long). I have a small child in my arms, a household to run. "I'm not sure that my demands are any less than yours," I tell him, and he must feel the harshness of my words, because he recoils.

"I never meant to imply that you didn't have demands. . . ."

I inform him that I'm going to visit my parents in Florida at spring break; perhaps we could meet there. Even as I say it, I'm having my doubts. But he says he'll see what he can do. I keep a mental list of what Jeremy's epitaph might read. "I'll only be a minute" is one possibility. "I'm under tremendous pressure" is another. "I'll see what I can do" is a third: that usually means he won't do it.

When we get off the phone, I want to call him back and say, "Let's just forget this," but I don't. I always want to call him back and say that, but I never do.

Every evening, the four of us have dinner together—Ramona and Andreas, Kate and I. Ramona tells me how she lost her hair. She was just a little girl, only six or seven, with long black hair, and she worked at a mill with her mother. One day while she was working, she was very tired and she must have dozed. She was jarred awake by the tug on her hair. It was caught in the mill. People rushed to her aid. Her mother came screaming, but nothing could be done. They couldn't stop the mill. The hair that was caught pulled right out of her head.

As she says this, Ramona tugs on the strands of hair that cover her bald spot. She was scalped, she tells me, just like that. Her own mother couldn't save her. Then she clutches her son to her, burying her face in his hair.

Abductions

Thirty-nine

A one-page newsletter from a group identifying itself as Uforum arrives in the mail. It announces a speaker who will discuss the magazine he publishes that his friends from Venus contribute to. I read in the blurb how the speaker "enjoys an ongoing friendship with people from Venus." I throw the newsletter away.

But a few weeks later another arrives, announcing a speaker who "will tell us about 4 days he physically lived on the planet Selo 5.9 light years from earth." Topics include: how he got there; what he did. What physical objects he brought back and what he learned. Cookies and juice will be served during the break.

In a small box I read that "If you are interested in the UFO abductee support group, you should call this number." I clip the phone number and walk around with it in my pocket for a few days. Then one morning I place a call to the editor of the newsletter, a woman named Ginger. I tell Ginger that I am a writer, interested in outer space and other planets and UFOs and abductees, and I ask her about her newsletter. She tells me that she is glad I am a writer and that I contacted her. The newsletter accepts all kinds of writing, including articles by extraterrestrials.

"You publish extraterrestrials?" I ask her.

Ginger informs me that articles from extraterrestrials arrive unsolicited in the mail, and she finds them in the "slush pile." She can recognize an article written by an ET because it is always signed, "Your brother in cosmic love." Ginger has friends from other worlds who live in human bodies. They write letters, though they do not sign them because they wish to remain in the planet earth "closet." "They don't think the way we do," she says. "When they have a thought or a decision to make, they don't think about themselves or even the planet. They think in terms of the entire solar system."

Ginger offers me all kinds of information. She says she is working on a pamphlet entitled "How to Recognize an Extraterrestrial." She says she's been hesitating about publishing it and feels this may have to do with the fact that the ETs are telling her that they do not want to be recognized. This is one of the most original procrastination excuses I have ever heard.

With some coaxing, however, Ginger explains to me how you recognize an ET. "It has to do with the metaphysical fourth-dimensional vibration level and learning to trust your own perception," she says. She knows when she's met an ET because she starts to get a clear pattern in her head of the individual afterward, and then she receives a message from him or her. Anyone who is a telepathic receiver will get a message.

Then suddenly Ginger grows distant, and I know the conversation is finished. Perhaps she has begun to wonder about the nature of my phone call. Perhaps a message is being sent to her. "If you want to attend a meeting of abductees," she informs me, "you must write a letter to Dr. Henry Z. Chesler, an ob-gyn and fertility expert in Long Beach." That afternoon I write to Dr. Chesler.

A week later I receive a reply. Dr. Chesler complains that in the past he has invited various people from the media and other individuals who have an interest in the UFO phenomenon. That these visits have, for the most part, been counterproductive, especially when dealing with the abductee support group. What Dr.

Chesler seems most bitter about is that no one has bothered to write him a thank-you note or make a phone call to the group.

"Why are you interested in UFOs?" Dr. Chesler writes me. "Are you in the process of writing a possible thesis about the UFO phenomenon? Do you think that in the past you may have had an abduction?"

Forty

A friend who runs a bookstore in Laguna has a man she wants to introduce me to. He's an investment banker, getting over "something." A very nice guy who wants to meet someone. My friend tells me he's rich and handsome and he reads books. I figure I may as well. We agree to meet at the bar at Las Brisas. He walks in and sees me sitting there. "Hello, Sandy," he says.

"Mary," I tell him.

We eat nachos and something called a *paco taco,* and he tells me that his life has just been blown apart. He was cheating on his girlfriend of eight years. In the middle of the affair, his lover's husband died of an epileptic seizure. The lover wouldn't see him anymore, and the girlfriend found out about the affair. "It's been a difficult time," he says.

"I can imagine," I tell him. I am coy, silent about myself, and besides he doesn't ask and has to be somewhere for dinner, so he asks if he can call me. "Can we have dinner next week?"

I rather like him. He's smart and not unattractive. I like his slicked-back hair, his sturdy build. He seems a bit distracted, but then he's getting over something. We've all got our baggage to drag around, don't we? I tell him sure, and he says he'll pick me up Wednesday after work.

When he arrives on Wednesday, Kate is playing on the floor with Andreas. He's building a city with blocks, and she's smashing it down. "Oh, that's sweet," the man says, smiling at the kids.

"Yes, they play nicely together."

"I mean it's nice that you let the maid have her kids here."

"Actually the little one is my kid."

He looks pale, somber. "Why didn't you tell me?"

"I was waiting for the right moment."

We have dinner in town and make small talk. Afterward I offer to pick up my tab. He thinks about it for a moment, then agrees. When I get home, I stay up, waiting to hear from Jeremy, waiting for him to phone. But he doesn't. That night and the next I go to bed weeping. In the morning I find a note slipped under my door. It reads: "Please don't cry so loud at night," and is signed: "A neighbor."

The next day I'm driving home from school when it starts to rain. The rain comes down heavily, and I put on my wipers. Almost as soon as I do, my left-hand wiper flips itself over and starts wiping the side of the car. I'm in the fast lane and can't see a thing. Opening the window, I reach for the wiper and try to turn it around. As I do this, I lose control of the car. The front end heads toward the guardrail, almost crashing into the median strip. It all flashes through my mind: the car smashing into the median; other cars piling up on me from behind. And what I see is Kate. Who will take care of her? Who will be there for her?

I manage to regain control of the car, turning it quickly so that it veers toward the next lane, where a truck is passing. I hear the screech of brakes, the angry honking of cars. I stay in my lane until I'm sure I can get over. Then I ease off the road, pull onto the shoulder. I turn off the engine and stay there, my head on the wheel, until the rain stops.

Forty-one

The Los Angeles chapter of the UFO abductee support group meets in a small clapboard bungalow near Brentwood. I spend a little time driving around, looking for the road. Then I see the cars and the lit-up house and park along the side street. As I am about to enter the house, two gatekeepers, both tall men, stop me. "Excuse me," one of them says, "but we need to know who asked you to come."

I hesitate for a moment. I read about this meeting in "Uforum." "Dr. Chesler invited me," I say. The two look at each other, then step aside to let me in.

I walk into what appears to be a party. Mostly people about my age, walking around with drinks in their hands. There are chips, crackers, and cheese on a table. Everyone is friendly, laughing.

I'm not sure what I expected to find. Kooks? Weirdos? Very obese or peculiar-looking people? Polyester and cranberry punch? These people could be friends. They're young and chatty. Some seem to know one another. It takes a while before I become aware of the whispering. A young man takes a woman aside. A girl with wavy brown hair comes up to me and asks if I am one of them. I say I am.

"Have you had an abduction?" she asks.

"I'm not sure."

"I wasn't sure for a while," she answers slowly, understanding my dilemma. "I knew something strange had happened to me, but I couldn't figure out what it was. I just felt different, that's all."

"How did you feel different?" I ask her.

"Well, for years I knew that something had happened to me. I mean, I was normal. I did well in school, I had boyfriends. But I kept remembering these things. . . ."

"Like what?"

"Like being taken somewhere, like having had things done to me."

She has lost her easy look and seems a little sad now, different from the girl I started talking to, as if that girl has drifted away. I begin to feel sorry for her. "Then I met Bud Hopkins, and I started to remember. . . ."

Bud Hopkins, a famous UFO abductee researcher, is scheduled to speak this evening. He has done extensive work with abductees and has special ways of testing and screening them. I am about to ask the girl what she remembers when she wanders off, and I soon see her talking in a corner with an older man.

But it is not long before a man in a plaid shirt comes up to me. He is quite attractive, with graying hair, and he asks me, straight out, if I am new and if I have had an abduction.

"I'm trying to remember . . ." I tell him.

"Yes," he says, "that's always the problem. You see, they blot out our memories. They have this way of making us forget what they've done to us. I've had experiments done on me. They cut my leg. I had something implanted in my nose. I had semen taken. For years I didn't remember it, but then the nightmares started. You see, memory bleeds. . . ."

"It bleeds . . . ?" I ask, taking all this in.

"Yes," he says. "Little pieces slip through. You remember this or that, and soon it starts to form a picture. Then I met Mr. Hopkins, and through hypnosis it all came back. Is that what's happening to you? Are you starting to remember?"

On June 24, 1947, a pilot named Kenneth Arnold was cruising in a private plane near Yakima, Washington, when he saw nine disk-shaped objects flying at a speed that he estimated was over seventeen hundred miles per hour. Later Arnold referred to their movement as that of "a saucer skipping over water." This event and Arnold's description of it represented—as David Jacobs, a Temple University history professor, pointed out in his book *The UFO Controversy in America*—not only the beginning of modern UFO sightings in the United States but also the origin of people's viewing UFOs as saucers.

Arnold was a deputy sheriff, a skilled pilot, a businessman, and a pillar of his community. His sightings were taken seriously by the Air Force. But Arnold was subsequently ridiculed for his use of the word "saucer." The idea of saucers flying around on their own evoked Alice's mad tea party more than anything to be taken seriously. Later Arnold would say, "If I saw a ten-story building flying around in the air, I would never say a word about it."

In the past fifty years, UFO sightings have become a staple of American discourse—be it mythic or real, by kooks or credibles. Sightings have been diverse and bizarre. In one incident surrounded by mystery and mystique, a spaceship was said to have crash landed in Roswell, New Mexico. The recent release of information that was classified during the cold war explained that what was taken for flying saucers was in fact spy planes on missions. The government preferred to let the American public believe there were flying saucers in our atmosphere rather than have it know of its top-secret intelligence missions.

I write this at the fiftieth anniversary of Roswell, and the manifestation has entered our mythology. In one ad campaign, Absolut Roswell, a flying saucer in a bottle of vodka, alights in the desert. Carl Jung was alive when Roswell happened (he died in 1961). Some of his final writings were about UFOs, which he didn't believe in. But he did believe that the circular or oblong shapes of UFOs are projections of the collective-unconscious symbol of wholeness and reflect our desire for integration. It is an integration that Buddhists understand.

On September 4, 1987, just days before I landed in California, President Ronald Reagan himself said, "I occasionally think how quickly our differences worldwide would vanish if we were facing an alien threat from outside this world, and yet, I ask, is not an alien force *already* among us?"

Along with UFO sightings have come reports of abductions. Though UFO abductees claim to have had implants put in their noses and legs, needles inserted in their penises and vaginas, sperm and eggs taken, there is no physiological evidence that anything has been done to them, though there may be scars.

No one actually remembers an abduction. The memory of it is blotted out, as the recent film *Men in Black* so comically showed. It is recovered later, through "flashbacks" and hypnosis. Recovered-memory syndrome has become an issue (and been debunked) in courts of law. The *Columbia Journalism Review* speaks of "bad therapists who implant memories not only of sexual abuse but also of such bizarre things as satanic cults, past lives, and alien abduction." Robert Jay Lifton, who has studied survivors of the Nazis and of Hiroshima, said in an interview on the *Today* show that clearly people who felt they'd been taken by aliens were survivors, but of what?

Another respected therapist and researcher of the paranormal, Dr. James Gordon, who met with alleged abductees, states in "The UFO Experience" (*Atlantic Monthly*, August 1991): "Early abuse, particularly sexual abuse, is also thought by some to be the cause of UFO-abduction memories; 'It's not my parents who abused me, but the aliens.' "

In a book, Bud Hopkins, this evening's speaker, defined the basic components of alien abductions: nighttime paralysis, the sense of a strange presence around your bed, an inability to rouse family members with your screams. The only evidence is the scars.

For about an hour I sit on the sofa, listening to the talk around me: nose implants that people sneezed out, memory blocks, the removal of sperm and eggs, missing time, ETs in plaid shirts and Oshkosh overalls. By now I feel an alien myself at this gathering. Then Bud Hopkins comes to the center of the small living room, and everyone huddles around him.

Hopkins wears a dark suit, a white shirt. He looks professional, serious. When he starts to speak, he is completely earnest. Hopkins tells us that he believes everything he hears. That is, he tries to convince the person who has had a strange experience to think he believes it, so that the person will tell his story. His chief research technique is to listen. And then, once he and his researchers determine that the person may be the victim of an abduction, he utilizes hypnotherapy in order to open the unconscious. "In this way," he informs us, "through hypnosis, memory is recovered."

"A man came to my house one day," Hopkins tells us. "He was a conservative southern businessman, a deacon in his church, who just rang the doorbell and said, 'I need to talk to you.' The man said that for years strange things had been happening to him. Small people cut his leg. He has a scar. He said he was driving home one night and suddenly found himself lost and his pants soaking wet. When he tried to make love to his wife, he was impotent for a time. Several months later he was abducted again, but this time he remembered it all. The ETs presented him with a child. They asked him to hold the child in a certain way. The ETs have a very ritualized ceremony of baby presentation, and this man knew the ceremony, though it has never been published, only told to researchers in minute detail.

"We are their laboratory animals," Hopkins continues. "They are using us in experiments, trying to understand what we are, perhaps reproducing us. Many instances have been recorded of sperm or eggs being taken. I have met with women who felt they had a child taken from them. Some women go through bizarre procedures to try to re-create the child. They get up in the middle of the night, leave home, searching for their lost child. One woman who lived in New York drove to Arizona, where she'd lived several years before, and she searched all the orphanages. She looked everywhere. She didn't remember what had happened to her, but she knew a child had been taken from her.

"There was one woman who went around with a pet monkey. It wore a diaper and sat on her shoulder. Even when she was pregnant with her second child, she kept the monkey on her shoulder.

Later, when interviewed, the woman told me about the missing-baby feeling and described a baby who looked like a shaved monkey. It was her husband who told me about the monkey she made him buy her. Another woman kept a doll with her at all times, treating it as if it were her child."

Hopkins tells a mesmerized room that he's had gentle people come to him with terrible stories. He heard one abductee say to another that he'd seen her before. Or at least he'd seen her head, alive on a shelf (à la the movie *Mars Attacks*). Hopkins tells of ordinary people coming to him with their Roswell stories. Soldiers are informed, "You have been the involuntary member of a secret Air Force experiment, and you must never tell anyone what you have seen, under pain of court-martial for treason."

An Australian Air Force pilot, named Valenti, reported an ET to his command, then disappeared from the face of the earth. One soldier was abducted, had a needle put up his penis, an implant in his thigh. Army doctors removed the implant. Every year he must come in for a physical. His records are top secret.

Hopkins concludes by saying that what happens to abductees is painful and terrifying, and ETs use memory blocks so that the abductee doesn't remember, but eventually memory starts to bleed.

Forty-two

My mother remembers things differently than I do. She remembers quiet Sundays, family picnics. I remember that nothing was ever right. That everything I did was wrong—the way I folded napkins, carried dishes. Someone was always yelling at me. When I grew up, a friend wanted to have buttons printed and distributed among our friends. Buttons that read: "I'm not mad at you, Mary." I remember other, more pleasant things. Running barefoot in the grass in my pajamas; eating fried chicken on a boat; my father, a smile on his face, hitting golf balls. "Always keep your head down," he said.

I remember lying in a basket in the back seat, a tornado chasing us down the road. My mother says that didn't happen but other things did. My clothes were never pressed, my lipstick was never right. I always needed a manicure. I dug holes into my flesh. Rage boiled inside me. My father shouting about lights being left on. My brother's hand being dipped into a scalding tub so he'd stop setting fires. These come to me in snatches.

Still, my mother says half of what I remember never happened. She says that the maid who got pregnant was Anka, not Herta, and that it was Herta who took my music box away. She says someone was always home when I got back from school. So why do I remember an empty house, unmade beds? Why do I remember my father's eyes turning red, his face like a dragon on fire?

When Jeremy and I first met and went to Tortola for a week, we stayed in a house that overlooked the sea, and every morning we wrote. I put out platters of fresh-cut fruit—papaya, mango. By noon we were on the beach, and in the evening we listened to conga bands. Then he started traveling again.

There was the letter Jeremy sent that November from Halifax. Wasn't it our first fall together? The trees in Central Park were a blaze of yellow, red, orange. I wore a wool scarf as I sat on a bench, reading what he wrote. *If I were ten years younger, I'd love you madly. But, alas, I am not, and so I will just love you.* I held that letter pressed to my heart. Underfoot I heard the crunch of autumn leaves.

Forty-three

At the New Age fair in Long Beach, a Terry Cole-Whittaker song is playing: "I'm a New Age Guy." Slogans abound: "If you don't change your direction, you'll wind up where you're headed." "Life's not a journey; it's a treasure hunt." "Creatures = Create Yours; Bountiful = Be It Full; Planet = Plan It!" I spend a weekend taking in all the booths: Crystal Clear; the Magical Dragon; the Mandala Vision; Super Kegel Demonstrations to strengthen the Kegel muscles in the groin (a dour, sexless woman in a gray suit is the demonstrator); the Cosmic Cheerleader; the man from Orion; the man in a three-piece suit who sells magical elixirs; the Rainbow Reader, who sees color in my name; Space Tomatoes that grow in the air; the Peaceful Warrior; the legless chair merchant; the light and sound show; Magical Fingers ("real fingers that massage your back"); the Unarians, who believe that in the year 2001 the Muons, who live on Myton, in the Pleiades, will pay a visit to earth; the Club Mud people; Power Places Travel Guides; Keiki, the Zen meditation center, where the monk has bad breath but is a beautiful being; the man who displays authentic crystal skulls (circa 20,000–4000 B.C.) but won't reveal their secret purpose; the art exhibit with paintings of van Gogh and da Vinci channeled through someone named José Rodríguez; SpaceWeights, crystal paperweights with space stations inside, made by a dentist's drill; Apache tears; the Hall of Intuitive Arts; those who draw electricity from the air.

We have come here to heal; we have all come to heal.

On the way home it rains, and I head straight for Ralph's.

Ralph can make neither head nor tail of my windshield wiper. "I just don't get it," he says, scrutinizing the parts he has strewn on the hood of my car and, with a magnifying glass, picking through the tiny screws and bolts. "It's got to be just the simplest thing." He's tried new parts, a new base, but all in vain. While Ralph peers at the wiper, his son stands behind him. "Maybe you don't need the wiper," the son says to me.

"She has to see," Ralph says, his eyes fixed on tiny bolts.

"That's right," I tell the boy. "I have to see." Kate's in her car seat, making impatient sounds.

"Try it now," Ralph says. He's changed the base, and when I flip it on it seems to work just fine. Then I drive through Laguna Canyon, and when I reach the ocean I spray on washer fluid, and as soon as I turn on the wiper, it flips over again.

I arrive a little late for the barbecue my neighbor Pat Dallas has invited me to at Smuggler's Cove. Willa has told me a little about Pat. She married an engineer and had four children. Then she married someone very rich. They divorced as well. Finally she found the love of her life in an Australian construction worker. They had a marriage service on the beach, after which, upon receiving his green card, her husband promptly left her.

Pat photographs nude men for *Playgirl* and gives me a copy of her book, *Dallas in Wonderland*. "Must be rough," she says to me, "raising a kid alone."

"Not easy," I tell her.

"Well, you've got your art," she says. "No one can take that away." At the barbecue, Pat takes snapshots of me and Kate. We mug for the camera, give each other wet kisses, exaggerated hugs. I tickle Kate under her arms so she'll smile. The contact sheets I will get are beautiful black-and-white beaming pictures I'll treasure always.

When I get home from the barbecue, Jeremy calls. He says he's trying to work out the logistics for spring break, which is still six weeks away. "Why don't you just do it?" I tell him. Why are there always logistics? "We could have spent months together, given the time we spend discussing logistics."

It's all so boring, really. Figuring out when to meet and how. Whenever we go somewhere, time gets whittled away. There's always some colleague he has to see, an unexpected lecture he has to give. Or his ex calls with some emergency about the boys.

"Five days," I tell him. "Just give me five days."

"I'll see what I can do."

"Just do it."

Restless, I start driving again. I go south with Kate, driving past San Diego, all the way to Tijuana. It is the first time I've crossed the border since 1983. It is immediately obvious which direction is more desirable. There are no lines leaving. But on the other side, coming into the country, the lines are very long. As I cross into Mexico, I think how I'd like to keep going south, head down to San Miguel, find Lupe and see her children again.

Instead I stop at a local market. It is replete with stands of papaya, mango, pineapple, corn, beans, a cornucopia of fruits and vegetables, hanging sides of beef and pork, coated with flies. I love the rancid, sticky-sweet smells of the Mexican market, the merchants shouting at the top of their lungs, slicing pink mango with a machete. I buy a mango, slice it thin, slip it into Kate's mouth. Her eyes open wide. For the rest of her childhood she'll beg for pineapple, tropical fruit. Now we wander about. She delights at the toys, the sombreros. I buy her an embroidered dress, a Mexican doll. We go to a taco restaurant for lunch.

When it is time to leave, we head out of town. The lines for customs are very long, but an official checking cars sees that I am a white woman with a child, and he waves me through.

Forty-four

ONE CALL ARRANGES ALL. That's what the big sign on the open book in front of Forest Lawn cemetery reads. My curiosity is piqued; I can't resist a visit to Forest Lawn. I drive through the wide-open gates, the largest wrought-iron gates in the world. Live geese waddle on the grounds at the entrance. There is a sign with a hand feeding ducks, an X through it—a no-no. At the Duck Pool, a fountain of iron storks sprays water into the sky. An "Inexpensive Mortuary" is advertised.

I enter the winding roads of the cemetery, which could just as easily be a park. Driving past an exact replica from the Pincio

Gardens in Rome of Pharaoh's daughter finding Moses in the bulrushes, I notice that there are no tombstones, only flat memorial markers. This was an important part of the builder's dream. That he would make a park as much for the living as for the dead, a place where artists could come and sketch, where happy children could see things they'd only read about in books.

I make my way slowly past upturned earth near newly dug graves. Fresh flowers dot the sloping green hills. No plastic flowers are permitted at Forest Lawn, and the florist at the entrance provides rather tired-looking fresh flowers: roses starting at $2.18; dyed blue and fuchsia daisies for $1.25. Signs near some of the new graves read: FLOWER THEFT IS A CRIME PUNISHABLE BY IMPRISONMENT.

I pull up in front of the entrance to the Great Mausoleum. I've heard that Trigger is buried here (he isn't; he's at the Roy Rogers and Dale Evans Museum in Victorville). There are no animals at Forest Lawn, I'm told. I've heard that a very rich woman is buried inside her red roadster. No one will vouch for that. But Gable and Lombard are in the Great Mausoleum, as are Jean Harlow and Sister Aimee Semple McPherson, the evangelist, who staged her own kidnapping, then killed herself with an overdose of sleeping pills.

I want to see their crypts, but I know it is tricky. My plan is to attend a viewing of *The Last Supper,* then sneak into the part of the mausoleum where they are buried. I was told this is possible if the guard is feeling relaxed. At the entrance to the mausoleum stand two little white plaster children with their dog, reading the "Builder's Creed," a huge sign carved into marble. I pause to read, in part: "I believe in a happy eternal life; I believe those of us who are left behind should be glad in the certain belief that those gone before who believed in him have entered into that happier life. I believe, most of all, in a Christ that smiles and loved you and me."

In the Memorial Court of Honor, I sit in a pew for a few moments, and soon music begins, a curtain is opened, and there, in all its splendor, is an exact replica of da Vinci's *Last Supper,* recreated in stained glass. It looms before me as a voice booms on. Afterward I wander down a corridor, where I am turned away when I plead, "I want to see Gable and Lombard." They guard their dead celebrities as if they are living.

Instead I walk through the "Westminster Abbey of the New World," where there are crypts no money can buy. The "Immortals" entombed beneath the stained-glass *Last Supper* include Gutzon Borglum, the American sculptor; Carrie Jacobs Bond, beloved writer of American folk songs; Dr. Robert Andrews Millikan, the physicist; Jan Styka, creator of *The Crucifixion;* Rufus B. Von KleinSmid, noted educator and humanitarian; and, of course, Dr. Hubert Eaton, the founder of Forest Lawn.

Hubert Eaton, the Dreamer, the Builder, creator of the Memorial Impulse, had a vision, which he realized in constructing his great cemetery. If you want a sense of what Eaton was like, you need only read Evelyn "Bites-the-Hand-That-Feeds-Him" (as he is referred to in *Mortuary Management*) Waugh's *The Loved One.* But it did not take much satire to capture this place. Forest Lawn is the masterpiece of West Coast facsimile. It has churches that exactly replicate the Church of the Hills, the New England meetinghouse where Henry Wadsworth Longfellow worshiped; the Old North Church of Paul Revere fame; the Wee Kirk o' the Heather, in Glencairn, Scotland, which contains mementos of Annie Laurie and her romantic love story.

I gaze at the Baptistry Doors, stop at the Court of David to look at what I have not seen since I was last in Florence: a reproduction of *David* (with fig leaf). Then I drive up to the Hill of the Ascension, where I look at the *Mystery of Life* statue. I walk down the hill, see vases of flowers on new graves. This is where the real human dramas are played out: a father who died just a year after his young son; a daughter, "Our Darling Deborah," with a bouquet of fresh roses; "Our Precious Mom," "Our Dearest Dad," lying side by side.

A car pulls up. A man approaches me. His car has New Mexico plates. He is young, rather handsome. "Excuse me," he says with a British accent, "but do you know how the lot numbers work around here? I'm trying to find this number." I look at his slip of paper. What is this person to him? I wonder. A relative, a friend? Someone he didn't know he missed until now?

"I'm sorry," I tell him. "I really don't know."

He thanks me. Then I see him climbing the hill. He climbs higher and higher. At last I see him pause. He takes out a pad of paper, begins to write. I observe him for a long time. For what is he grieving? Whom has he lost? And what is he writing down? I watch until I know it is rude for me to watch any longer, then I get in my car.

I drive down past the Vale of Memory to Vesperland; turning right at Graceland, I find myself pausing before a heart-shaped drive called Babyland. At the base of the heart stands a bronze statue—a naked baby with outstretched arms. I pause here, looking at the graves of dead babies, tiny tots. On the grave markers I see carved "Our Precious Angel," "God's Little Gift," and epitaphs like "the one we waited for now gone." Then I get in my car, drive up the slope of Everlasting Love, and rush back home.

Forty-five

I'm invited to a barbecue by a friend of Catherine's sister. There's a cement mixer on the lawn. The man who lives here is a firefighter on constant call. Indeed, I am told he might get called at any moment, because there are brush fires in the hills above Laguna. He holds back his two pit bulls when I walk in. I'm nervous about putting Kate down on the floor.

Ribs slathered in sauce are cooking on the grill. *Top Gun* is on TV. Assorted antlers and guns hang from the walls. The phone keeps ringing. He tells me about the blazes up in the hills. He takes crews of prisoners with him to fight the fires; if they are good, they may qualify for work release. The pit bulls are put into a pen, and I let Kate crawl around. Ribs and chicken and coleslaw are served in big bins, and everyone fills a plate.

When I go back inside, a basketball game is on. I hear someone say, "Who's winning the game? Their niggers or ours?"

Another issue of "Astrology and Psychic News" arrives, and Andreika, the witch, runs an ad.

> I will cast a spell for you. Listen to what I say. Do what I tell you. I exist in the fourth dimension. I can vanish from the present and appear beside someone without them knowing it. I can cast a spell to make one love another, or cause a person to change his mind, or disintegrate a relationship or bring two people together. I can do these things because I have the combined powers of my mother who was a sorcerer and my father who was a warlock.

I am Andreika, the witch, and I can change the course of destiny. Pay me and I shall cast a spell in your favor. Send me your most important desire and I shall work my powers in your favor.

I read the thank-you letters that accompany the ad. Dreams come true; wishes are granted. One woman has her rent miraculously lowered, another wins the Ohio state lottery; a wayward husband returns, a court case is favorably settled, a sick child is healed.

I cut out the coupon. For a while I contemplate dropping the fifteen dollars plus postage into the mail.

I catch Jeremy late one afternoon as he is racing out the door. He says he's in a hurry; he'll call me later. "Where are you going?" I ask, knowing that rushed tone. It's as if he's got something he's not quite right about, as if he is slightly ashamed.

He says he's going to get a dog for his son Evan. "Evan needs some responsibility, something to take care of."

"Yes, I'm sure he does. Are you going to the pound?"

"Well, no, not exactly." I decide to press him.

"Just what kind of dog are you getting?"

"Well, Evan wanted an Akita. . . ."

An Akita. In my old neighborhood on the West Side there was a shop called Akitas of Distinction (they went out of business when the *Village Voice* ran an article called "Akitas of Deception"). I used to stop in there from time to time and check out the dogs. "What's it cost, fifteen hundred dollars?"

"Oh, no," Jeremy says. "Just twelve hundred."

I try to control my anger. He has not given one penny to our daughter since she was born; he has rebuffed my requests for two hundred dollars a month for weekend help. Twelve hundred dollars would be six months' child care. It would enable me to take a shower and maybe prepare for school on Sunday.

"That's a very expensive dog," I tell him.

"Yes." His voice grows defensive. "But it's what Evan really wanted. And he needs the responsibility."

"He could start with his sister, couldn't he?"

"Well, it's an expensive dog, that's true, but I've looked into it quite a bit." An Akita is a designer dog, but Jeremy has found the perfect way to justify this purchase.

"It's an easy dog to give away," he says.

Project Evacuation

Forty-six

Wanda phones to say that Ashtar is assembling his light workers all over the planet and will meet with them on Friday night. Can he be in all those places at once? I want to ask. How does he do this? Galaxy-at-a-glance? You have been chosen, Wanda tells me.

The earth-based unit will be meeting in Laguna Hills, and I tell her I will come. I make arrangements for Kate, and on Friday evening, under a blue moon, I head up to Top of the World. The road is dark, and there are no cars, almost no lights on in the houses. Where have all the people gone?

The house is immaculate. A few of the regulars are there. I recognize Carl, the black muscular therapist, and Marcia, the decorator. A group of newcomers sit statuelike, motionless, expectant. The women wear polyester leisure suits, the men sports shirts and khakis. Most of the women are blond, with slightly bouffant hairdos. This looks like a movie set from the 1950s. *Ozzie and Harriet* could be filmed right in this living room, only as if they lived in a wax museum.

Wanda sits in the middle, wearing, as always, her pink jumpsuit and flying-saucer earrings. A plate of chocolate chip cookies is on the table, a bowl of punch on the sideboard. I am offered refreshments by our host, but I decline. They have been waiting for me. "Mary is late as usual," Wanda says as I take my place, cross-legged, on the floor. "We know why this is so." Wanda smiles and I smile back, embarrassed to be singled out in this way. "Is this because Mary is unsure? Because she is resistant?" Wanda looks at me, as if waiting for an answer. She is right, of course, about why I am late, but I cannot tell her this is so. I am relieved when she answers for me. "Mary is late because she has a small child to raise and because she has too much work to do. So we must forgive her her lateness. She is learning to make her way."

Wanda gives me another smile, and again I smile back. "Now," Wanda says, "Ashtar is ready to join you, and I wish you a safe and pleasant flight." She closes her eyes. Her lids begin to flutter. Then Ashtar speaks through her. He says what I have heard him say before. Use the earth to stabilize yourself. Hug a tree, kiss the earth, feel the breeze. Let the energy expand into the smell of flowers, but then be prepared to let it go. Don't hold on to anything. What you hold on to, you destroy. You must let everything on this planetary plane go in order to reach the next level.

Then Ashtar tells us that Project Evacuation is about to be implemented. That it is almost time for us to leave. We should begin to put our affairs in order, for the end—or the beginning, which is how we must learn to see it—is near. "It is only a matter of weeks now," Ashtar says. There is a veritable sigh in the room, a blend of excitement and fear. "I know you have your concerns," Ashtar says in his squeaky voice. "And I want you to express them. Today you may ask me whatever is on your mind."

A man in a button-down shirt, wearing a tie, who looks as if he works for a software company, wonders how he should prepare for the journey. Ashtar informs him that by coming here he has already begun his preparation. A woman inquires nervously about children, and Ashtar assures her that children will be welcomed in the planets that are being prepared when Armageddon comes and we are beamed up. The light workers and their families will be the first to leave.

I ask Ashtar if I can take anything with me from this planetary plane. He has answered the children question, but I am thinking of the little things I wouldn't want to do without—a good book, my journal, my favorite mug. He seems slightly disgruntled by my question and informs me that no earthly objects except for our souls can make such a journey, but on the astral plane we will not need books or clothes or food. We will need only the spirit.

I look at Wanda, her lids fluttering, her palms resting neatly in her lap. "Why have you chosen Wanda to be your vessel?" I ask.

Ashtar is silent and seems to be pondering this. Then he says, "Wanda must answer that for herself. I cannot speak for her."

Ashtar leaves and Wanda opens her eyes. She refers to herself in the third person. "Wanda," she says, "came into a body with no childhood. She experienced incest in her first soul and then searched to heal. As she searched, she transcended the planetary and astral levels and reached the fourth level of consciousness, where she made contact with the extraterrestrial fleet. Now she wants to see the divine love in all our faces. She wants to experience the light in us all. Wanda now wants to connect, and she will connect by bringing you to Ashtar, who has offered his guidance and his divine love. She has found the way to heal, and she offers it to you."

Then Wanda drops her eyes and is silent. Everyone in the room breathes a sigh.

Forty-seven

I've come to dread the rain. Whenever I get in the car, I check the weather report. I worry that my windshield wiper will flip and I won't be able to see. But the weather promises to be nice today as I drive north up the coast. I'm not sure how far I'll get. Maybe

Big Sur. Maybe not quite so far, though in fact Kate and I get pretty close.

I stop somewhere along the coast highway. There are paths we can hike through. Horses graze in the valley below, along the seaside. We linger there most of the day. I give Kate a picnic of cut-up banana, peanut butter that she licks off my fingers. When I let my eyes gaze at the sea, she wades into a patch of poison ivy. I give a holler, scooping her up, and she slips her hand onto my breast. Later I will develop a most annoying case of poison ivy, but Kate, it seems, is immune.

It is dusk as we head back south. We drive for a long time, but then, near San Luis Obispo, I see storm clouds overhead. Already a light rain has begun to fall. "Let's spend the night somewhere," I tell Kate. The Madonna Inn is nearby.

A few rooms are available. They are expensive, but I've got the credit card. It's a splurge I know I shouldn't make, but I can't resist. We check out the Safari Room, which is done in *faux* tiger and zebra skin; the Tack Room (too many whips); the Old World Room (too fancy); the Crystal Room (too breakable). Each of these rooms is what Mrs. Madonna sees in her dreams. She has a vision, then she executes it. I can't help but think of Forest Lawn and much of what I've seen since I've come to California, this place of dreamers. We peer into the Cave Man Room, which is too primitive for a mother and daughter, and in the end I opt for the Old Mill.

The Old Mill Room has a miniature working mill wheel above the bed and water churning around the upper moldings of the room. Kate and I have a bite in the dining room, decorated in neo-bordello, with gilded grapes dangling from the fixtures, then play with the mill until bedtime. Exhausted, I am asleep as soon as my head hits the pillow, but in the middle of the night something jars me. I wake to see the room brightly lit, the mill churning; water splashes onto the bed. Gleefully Kate dips her hands in and out of the water, drenching me.

We stop at Jimmy's place in Malibu on the way back, and Willa takes us up Tuna Canyon to see the magic horse. We drive halfway, then park and hike. As we walk, I can see where the fires have burned the side of the canyon. The fires cause erosion, the rains come and bring the mud; that's the basic equation for Malibu. "You see where there's no growth around the houses?" Willa points to houses that sit on bald hills. "That's so the fires won't reach them. Sometimes the firefighters won't even come into some of these canyons. They can get trapped. People up here have to fight their own fires sometimes. But you know," she says, "they have these fire experts. People who know the properties of fire. Which way it will blow. How to make it turn around and go another way. They tell the people here what to do."

I see whole hillsides that have been scorched. We walk in silence for a while. Then Willa says, echoing what Patricia Holland had said a few months before, "I don't think you're going to be here long."

"You don't? Why not? I was planning on staying."

"I don't think so," Willa says. "It doesn't seem right to me."

With Kate toddling at my side or resting in Willa's arms, we hike up a winding road until we come to a rise where a pure white horse stands. "That's Quasar," Willa says.

Kate, her pockets filled with carrots, rushes to the thirty-year-old horse. The magic horse eats out of her hand.

The same friend who fixed me up with the man who thought my name was Sandy fixes me up with Valentine. I want to say no, but who can resist a name like that. I get dressed up to go out: a sundress with straps. But Valentine picks me up and takes me to his place.

Valentine lives in a one-room studio at the back of a 1940s hotel that has been converted into apartments. He is making us dinner—brown rice, halibut, an excellent summer salad with crispy leaves, yellow peppers. Valentine is very East Coast, easy to talk to. He shows me his beautiful photographs, and I admire them.

Then we sit down to eat, and over candlelight, with the champagne, Valentine takes out a clipboard and proceeds to write down every word I say. This bothers me and I mention it, but he says it's the only way he can really concentrate.

As I take a bite of food and compliment him on his cooking, he pauses, pencil poised against his face. "You know," he says, "there were never any seconds in my house, because my mother always served all the food on my plate at once." He thinks about this, then scribbles it down.

After dinner I say I need to get back. I make the baby excuse, but for a moment we stand on his patio, gazing at the stars. I decide to ask my usual question. "Valentine, have you ever been visited?"

He says he has. "Just once. I was sitting by a swimming pool with a friend in Hollywood, and a force came down to the other end of the pool—the deep end. It went swish, then straight up. We couldn't really see it, but we both knew it was there."

When I get home, I phone Jeremy, who isn't there. I leave a message, but he doesn't call back. The next day he phones from his office. "You know," I say, "you almost never answer your home phone anymore. And you don't call me at night. Why is that?"

"I don't want to disturb you."

"That never bothered you before. And you don't call me from home."

"What is this?" Jeremy asks, irritation rising in his voice. "The third degree?"

Forty-eight

Anaheim was just an orange grove when Walt Disney first set his sights there. Walt had a vision and he needed space, cheap land. Originally he thought he'd build his theme park across from Disney Studios in Burbank. He could be seen on quiet Sunday afternoons, wandering the perimeters of a weed-filled lot. But before long that lot wasn't big enough for his ideas.

It was in 1953 that he saw the site for the current Disneyland. "In those days," Disney said, "it was all flat land—no rivers, no mountains, no castles or rocket ships."

Laura, a secretary in the English Department, says that if I've never been to Disneyland with Kate, she'd love to take us. This seems like a good way to see it, so we choose a date and Laura picks us up.

Almost as soon as we get there, I'm exhausted. I can't bear the endless standing in line for each ride. I can't stand all those people smiling at me. Goofy comes over to Kate and gives her an autograph. We spend most of the morning in Fantasyland, sailing with Nana through Never-Never-Land, spinning in the Mad Hatter's Tea Cups. We splash down Pirates of the Caribbean, then the lines get too long and we decide to head over to New Orleans Square, where Laura has made a lunch reservation.

Blue Bayou is basically a phony swamp—Spanish moss hanging from the ceiling, water and swampy creatures everywhere in a huge, dark blue room. It feels hot, boggy, claustrophobic as we settle in and order our jambalaya. The lunch arrives, and there's too much of it; it's too spicy.

Then Laura tells me that she's glad I've come to California. "It's a good thing you're here. I came to heal as well."

"Heal from what?" I ask, but already I've got that sinking feeling in my gut.

"Well, we all have something to get over, don't we?"

"Yes, I suppose so. . . ."

"You see, with me it was my brothers. My mother, she just couldn't control them. . . ." Then she begins telling me about her family of ten siblings and about the sexual abuse she endured at the hands of her brothers. Her mother knew about it but said she could do nothing.

The jambalaya is hot and spicy, the room hot and oppressive. The Spanish moss seems to touch my sweaty arms. When we get outside after lunch and find ourselves back on Bourbon Street, I tell Laura I want to head to the quieter climes of Frontierland. We take a paddleboat up the Mississippi, and then, just after we witness a shootout with Indians and are waved at by a robot Jim, the runaway slave, I tell Laura I'm ready to head home.

I am supposed to go to a book signing at Waldenbooks for my new book. At the mall, tables for the signing are set up in the midst of a lawn and garden show. Amid the lawn spreaders and the hammocks and a putting green, there are books, but no customers.

At the next table is a woman named Elizabeth Cather, who writes romances. She is seventy-five years old, and at first I am put off by her, but since we are in the middle of a mall with very few book buyers, we start to chat. Some little girls come over to her table and talk with her for a long time. When they leave, I say to her, "They love you."

And she replies, "Because I love them."

Her life, Elizabeth tells me, has been a celebration of love. At eighteen, she saw a man walking by and knew that this was the man she was supposed to spend her life with. They were married for forty-six years and shared a life of perfect love. Then he died, ten years ago. She puts him in each of her books. "It's always a comfort for me," she says, "to have him there." When he was dying, she said to him, "How will I know where you are going? We need a password," she said. And he put his arms around her. "We don't need any password," he said.

I burst out crying. Elizabeth looks at me. "Why are you crying?"

Because it's a beautiful story, I tell her.

Jeremy doesn't call all week, and Ramona agrees to stay the weekend so I can go to Vegas again. I promise to be back by Sunday morning, and early Saturday I set off on the desert road. I drive straight through the heat of the desert and arrive at the Riviera. Irish is working the wheel, and when he sees me he gets his pit boss to fill in.

"Lady Luck," Irish says when he sees me. "What're you doing back here?"

"I want to try and win again," I say.

"Dumb broad," Irish says, with no irony. "Come on, I'm gonna buy you the best corned beef sandwich you ever tasted."

I haven't eaten a corned beef sandwich since my father brought cold cuts home on Sunday mornings when I was a girl. Just the mention of corned beef brings tears to my eyes. I'm not sure if Irish sees this, but he takes me by the arm, leads me through the darkened casino, winding wormlike, into a room of mirrors and tables and men speaking on telephones at their tables.

He orders two corned beef sandwiches on rye, with Swiss and sauerkraut, and two black cows. "I can't eat that," I say, feeling sick in the pit of my stomach and wanting to race home, if one can race for six hours.

"You'll eat. You need to eat something."

When the food comes, he watches me intently as I gobble it down. Then he says, "You were hungry. I knew that right away."

"How'd you know?"

"When people start to lose, they get hungry. It's a look in the eye."

"Am I losing?"

"You tell me."

I shrug. "I might be."

"Look," Irish says, "I don't want to pry, I'm not that kind of a guy, but you're a nice girl. I know that about you." Before I can ask him how he knows, he waves me away. "It's in your eyes. Anyhow, let me tell you something. Gamblers have tells. That's the little gestures they make when they're winning, when they're bluffing, when they're hedging their bets. You play with somebody long enough, you get to know what it means when so-and-so taps his forehead or rubs his nose. That's how I get to know people. I look for the tells. I'm an expert at human observation."

"And?"

"And you're in trouble. I can see that. Not 'cause you drove here from L.A. Thousands of people do that every day. But you got something sad in your face. You belong somewhere else."

I finish the corned beef sandwich, amazed at how I wolfed it down. "I guess you're right."

"Whatever's bugging you, let me tell you—I learned this a long time ago—if it's bugging you, it ain't good for you. You know what I'm saying?"

"Not exactly."

"Yes you do. It ain't good for you."

Irish comps my meal, then takes me to the blackjack table, where he teaches me a little about being a systems player, none of which makes much sense to me. I win a hundred bucks, mainly because Irish is telling me what to play. "Good; now you're ahead. Quit, go to sleep, get an early start in the morning." He gives me a little nod, a pat on the cheek.

After Irish leaves me, I go back to the blackjack table, where I think I know what to do, but though I'm ahead for a little while, I lose my first hundred in a few hands, to a dealer who seems to feel sorry for me. Thinking I'll do better on roulette, I blow some more on the wheel, and I end the night dropping coins in the slots.

There's a grandmother next to me, with white leather gloves, and she's doing a two-fisted job at two machines. From time to time I hear that thick ripple of coins clanging into the cup. Maybe I can pay for my weekend, even get some extra child care this way. I keep thinking I'll hear that sound from my own machine before the night is over, but I never do.

When I get to Laguna, Kate and Ramona greet me in the garden. I'm glad to be back. I don't want to go anywhere ever again. I check the answering machine. There are two messages from friends back home, but nothing from Jeremy. I was sure he would call. I ask Ramona if there were any other calls. There were, but none from him.

That night there is a full moon over the Laguna cliffs. I head out after dinner, telling Ramona I've got something to do. Usually I walk here in the afternoon, but now it is dark despite the full moon and the path is hard to follow. The wind blows hard off the Pacific. I am walking like a madwoman along the cliffs, when I hear someone call my name. It is loud and clear. *Mary,* someone calls to me, and then again, just as clear, *Mary.* I turn and look. I pause and wait again. I am sure I heard someone calling to me. But no one is there.

Forty-nine

The phone rings early the next morning and I hear the crackling of long distance, an international operator asking if I'll accept a collect call from Guadalupe Martinez. "Lupe," I shout into the phone, "Lupe, where are you?"

She tells me she's in Queretero, helping raise her grandchildren. I tell her I'm raising my daughter in California and I tickle Katie so that she laughs into the phone. "So now we are old," Lupe says.

"No," I tell her. "I feel very young."

"I'm raising my grandchildren," Lupe says as if she can't believe it. "What does your husband do?"

"I'd called because I wanted you to come here." I pause. "I don't have a husband."

Lupe doesn't laugh, which I imagined she'd do. Instead she says, "So you are just like me."

"Yes, I suppose I am."

"Things could be worse," she says, and now I hear that laughter in her voice.

"I called because I wanted you to come here."

There is silence, a sigh. "I'd have to bring some children, two or three. . . ." Her voice trails off.

"It's all right," I tell her. "I'm really doing all right on my own." As I say this, I know it's true.

Elizabeth Cather belongs to a fifteenth-century Hindu sect called the Absolute. She informs me of this when I go to visit her in the trailer park where she lives. Her religion, Elizabeth explains, is carried in her inner heart. "It's the furthest thrust of the human mind into the unknown."

On a whim, I called Elizabeth, who invited me to tea at the Grove Trailer Park. When I arrive, Elizabeth is wearing a pink dress with ruffles, her hair neatly combed. There are trinkets, mementos, everywhere. Pictures of her husband of forty-six years. We sit down, and Elizabeth wastes no time on small talk. "I've learned to stop grabbing life by the throat and demanding from it," she told me. "Instead just open the door and let the light in. There's no reason to live in the dark.

"In my Hindu teachings, there are three levels—being, consciousness, and rapture. I'm living a life of rapture now." I know it's a bit hokey, but I like Elizabeth. She has this big wide grin, and what she says seems to make some sense.

"Let me tell you a story of an unlived life," she says. "My mother adored my father. They were married and they went to Europe for a six-month honeymoon. When they returned, my mother was excited about the prospect of decorating the house they had bought just before leaving. But as she walked up the front steps, chintz curtains hung in the windows, sofas and chairs could be seen. The young bride peered in. Surely, she thought, this was some mistake. But it was not. While they were away, her mother-in-law had decorated the house and set up a wing for herself and her unmarried daughter. For the rest of her married life, my mother was never alone. She begged my father, pleaded with him, but he could not send his mother and sister away. One night they were making love. They couldn't make love in their own room, because the mother would listen at the door and say things like 'dirty' or 'filthy.' So they slunk down to the living room, and just at the moment when their passion was reaching its height, my grandmother flung open the door and shouted at them, calling them filth and scum. I was born nine months after that night, and my parents were never together again as a married couple. My mother was never right after that; she was never of this world. She hardly even knew I existed. She went through life like a dreamer."

When Elizabeth's father was supposedly dying of pneumonia, her mother gave all their money—$200,000—to a preacher and went to live on a commune. The father lived impoverished for twelve years after that, and Elizabeth never saw her mother again. They tried to find her, to get her out of the commune, but they never did. She died in a pauper's ward in a hospital.

Elizabeth looks at me, breathless. "I'm not sure why I told you that story, but I want you to see why love is so important. Why loving someone is important."

Elizabeth reaches across, touching my hands. "I see good things for you, Mary. You are ready for the gift of love."

I'm not sure she's right, but this doesn't seem to be the time, or the place, to argue.

Fifty

When you cross the moat into the castle at Medieval Times, you are handed a crown. The crowns come in red, yellow, green, blue, black, and white, and the color of your crown represents that of the knight you are rooting for. Busloads of Chinese tourists, overweight women from the Midwest, drunken men, a busload of blacks, as well as the generic Disneyland tourists, all parade around in their crowns. A woman tries to give Willa a red crown and me a blue one, but I insist that we take the same color. Some people have bent the points of their crowns down—a minor attempt at individuality.

We avoid the woman who tries to sell you your family coat of arms and push on through the thousands of tourists that they process each night, to reach our seats in the section of the blue crowns around the jousting pit.

A wench in a peasant blouse, drawn tight across the top of her breasts, tosses half a chicken and a baked potato on our silver plates. Knives and forks are offered, but most attendees eat with their hands, ripping the chicken apart, chomping on the potato. Our steins are filled with ale.

The master of ceremonies welcomes us in Elizabethan English

to his court, asks us to imagine we are in Arthurian England, and says we are his most ennobled guests for the evening and our wishes shall be his commands and those of his attending wenches and his queen, the fair Guinevere, who executes a small curtsy. Willa cocks her head. "I know that guy," she says.

"You do?"

She nods. "I used to work with him at the Playhouse." He is a Laguna Beach Moulton Playhouse reject, a failed Shakespearean actor, who should be doing Lear. Instead he expounds on the evil Green Knight, "a wart on the nose of chivalry, from the town of Leon, a cesspool, a pestilence, a plague." He is to be destroyed, devoured, eviscerated. Cheers ring out; the joust is on.

We try to imagine reciting the same tired script night after night, rather than acting Macbeth. When the knights are introduced—the red, then the yellow, the blue, and so on—their respective sections rise to their feet and offer collective roars, cheers, shouts of *Kill, Kill*. Aging stuntmen, Willa says, as we watch them jab at a target, run their lance past an opponent.

We watch the joust for an hour or so, then decide we can't stand it anymore. We sneak out of Medieval Times, laughing, after having stolen the program we were supposed to buy.

As we head off into the night, two clay horses in the fake paddock at the TraveLodge next door seem to look our way.

Recovered Memory

Fifty-one

At spring break, I head to Florida to see my parents and Jeremy. After weeks of negotiating, we have agreed to meet on that neutral ground. During our last phone call, I told him I was nervous about this trip.

"I miss you," he told me.

"I miss you too."

I have not seen him in three months, but I know from our conversations that we are both ready to try again. I arrive a few days early and stay with my wary parents. They do not ask, they do not dare interfere, but their eyes tell me: Do you think this is a good idea?

If this is what you want, my mother says to me at one point. If this is what's best for you and Kate.

I tell her it is. She listens, nodding, her lips pursed together, not daring to say anything more.

I am in Florida three or four days before Jeremy is supposed to arrive. This gives me time to wander the shore with Kate. We explode jellyfish with sticks and keep a look out for dolphins. The day Jeremy is to arrive with his two boys, we drive to the airport. His plane is right on time. He stands flanked by his teenage sons, and I stand between my parents, our daughter in my arms.

He looks very good to me. Very good. Too good really. Almost immediately I know something isn't right. "How are you?" he asks me, bending over to give me a kiss, but I step away. Jeremy looks surprised but then must think it has something to do with my parents. But as he stands smiling at me, racket in hand, I have a sinking feeling. It's vague, but I know things are not as they should be. I look at his khaki suit, his duffel, his beard. *What is wrong with this picture?* I was never very adept at that test in school, and now I rack my brain.

What was it Irish said about how a gambler has tells? Those little signs that give it all away. The way they tug on an ear, rub their nose. When you live with somebody, when you know him for years, you get to know his quirks. Jeremy won't eat oatmeal, hates crowds, and prides himself on not having been to a barber in over twenty-five years. I cut his hair when he visited in the fall and again over the holidays. His ex-wife did it for years before that.

Now I look at him. At his tanned face and pressed khaki suit. At his trimmed hair and beard. I take a step back and remember the voice of that woman on the phone New Year's Eve. Suddenly I see as clearly as I have ever seen. "Who cut your hair?" I ask him. "Who cut your hair?"

Over the five days we are together, I ask this question repeatedly, and there is never any answer that makes sense. "Various people," is one of the responses I get. I ask yet again who called on New Year's and why he broke our Valentine's plans. One of the boys, the younger one, mentions that Sigrid knows how to drive their father's new car. Sigrid? I ask. Is she around?

Finally the older son says to me, "Don't you know anything? Don't you know what's going on here?"

"I guess I don't," I tell him. "I guess I don't really know."

One evening after dinner, Jeremy and I take a walk along the shore and I confront him. "Tell me about Sigrid. I have the right to know."

"It's nothing," he tells me. "She's just a holding pattern." I picture Sigrid, a 747, circling Newark Airport. "Don't you know that you're the one I love?"

Perhaps for myself alone I wouldn't leave him. But suddenly I am thinking of my daughter. I am thinking of Kate. Sometime in the last year I made the decision that I'd never hurt her. Now I'm deciding that no one ever will. "You didn't call your sons when we went to Tortola, did you?"

Jeremy laughs, thinking I have some form of attention disorder. "What's that got to do with anything?"

"I just didn't think about it much at the time. That you didn't call them. But now I do."

The flight back to California seems endless. I am numb on the first stage of the journey, staring out the window. Mountains, river, desert drift by. How was it that I didn't see what was in front of me? How could I have been so blind? I change planes in Dallas. Clouds go by, mountains pass below. On these long flights when I hold my daughter in my lap, my arms ache.

As the plane is about to land, Kate begins to cry. Her ears are hurting. She wakes, sobbing, in my lap. The stewardess comes by, and I say, "Her ears hurt."

"Here, honey," the stewardess says, holding Kate's bottle out to her. "Take this; it will help you."

Kate takes the bottle and sticks it in her ear.

When I get back to school, Laura hands me a message. A reporter from *The Daily Planet* wants to interview me. I envision Clark Kent, whipping off his glasses in a phone booth. There are also several messages from Jeremy, who also left them at home. For some reason the message from *The Daily Planet* doesn't surprise me (though in fact the reporter turns out to be from *The Daily Pilot*). Jeremy's messages do.

I stopped speaking to him during his Florida stay. When I

took him to the airport, I told him not to call me again. Like a puzzle, the pieces of what had happened fell into place. Our Valentine's plans had been canceled because Sigrid was living in Jeremy's house. So how could I go there? Of course she had called on New Year's. Of course she had been in the picture all along. I just refused to acknowledge it.

I do not return any of Jeremy's calls. Nor do I return the reporter's call. Nor do I return any messages, for that matter. My phone rings, and I do not respond. I ache with loneliness, but I will not answer the phone.

Then late one night, I decide to make a phone call. In "Astrology and Psychic News" I find the number of the psychic who helps you find your dog. I recognize the exchange, and it isn't far from where I live. After everyone is asleep, I pick up the phone and dial. I let it ring four, five times, then I hear the somewhat gravelly voice of an older woman, a smoker's voice, say, "Can I help you?"

"Yes," I tell her. "I've lost my dog. He ran away about three days ago and I can't seem to find him." My voice is quivering, and at the thought of the little dog I don't have, tears well up in my eyes.

"What is the dog's name?"

The dog's name. What is the dog's name? I give it the name of the only dog I know. "Hiroshi, his name is Hiroshi. He's a Japanese dog."

"What does your dog look like?" she asks me.

I describe for her a creature I have never seen but imagined over and over in my mind. It is a dog I seem to know only too well. "It's a brown-and-white dog with a brown patch over its eye, a fluffy coat. An Akita puppy." Closing my eyes, I see Hiroshi, the dog Jeremy bought for his son, the dog that would have bought me child care for half a year. Picture this dog, I tell myself. Small, with a white-and-brown coat, sad brown eyes, big clumsy paws. Gnaws on the molding if locked up in a room, huddles in corners.

"A door must have been left open," I tell the woman on the other end. "Somehow the dog escaped." I tell the woman that I miss my dog very much.

She listens attentively, in silence. I imagine that she is envisioning Hiroshi, crouched in a corner, scared. That she sees him in a garage or in a house that isn't mine.

Instead she says into the phone, "You don't have a dog." And she slams the receiver down. I am left, holding the receiver in my hand, listening to the dial tone. You don't have a dog, she said. And, of course, she is right. I don't.

Fifty-two

The reporter from *The Daily Pilot* sounds pleasant on the phone, and I agree to see her. She wants to talk to me about my new book, my life, and I sit through the interview in a daze. I am so tired I think my head will burst. Though she is kind and thoughtful, I don't want to answer her questions. I stare at the spinning tape recorder and think I'm not sure how I can go on. Even as I speak to her, my arms feel heavy from holding Kate. How can I manage this alone? And now I know I really am alone. Not just physically, but in my heart as well.

The Sunday after the interview happens to be Mother's Day. Kate wakes at six, knocks over her food tray, screams as I try to take a shower, and leaves me sobbing on the floor by eight A.M., the whole day ahead of me. I cannot go on, I tell myself. Somehow I know as I grope around on the floor in my torn sweatpants, picking up the globs of cereal, that I've reached the end of the line.

That is when I hear my gate clang. Looking up, I see a woman I know from somewhere but cannot place. Dressed in a pink spandex outfit, with a dozen pink roses in her arms, she is making her way up my walk. She knocks on the door and finds me in tears, food all over the floor. "I just wanted to wish you a happy Mother's Day," the reporter from *The Daily Pilot* says, and I fall into her arms, sobbing.

"Now you just relax," she says as she makes a pot of coffee. She hands me the newspaper, plucks up the baby, and puts her in her playpen, with piles of toys. Then she proceeds to clean my house. I sit mesmerized, watching this stranger make my beds, scramble eggs.

As I watch her scrubbing the muck off the floor, giving Kate a rinse-off bath, something begins to shift inside me—a small view into the world as a better place than I had imagined until now. A germ of the idea begins to grow—that I can turn this around. There will be no easy answers, no simple solutions. But perhaps in the end there are miracles. All my time with channelers and New Age practitioners has led me to believe I can reinvent myself; I can begin again yet one more time.

In the end I know what I've come to believe in. It's another California cliché, but I've come to believe in myself.

That evening I make the winding drive up to Top of the World, where Sharon and Randall from Project Evacuation live. Since tomorrow is the day when the world will be destroyed, the light workers are being assembled. It is important, the caller told me, that we are all clear about our plan. Ashtar has summoned this special meeting, which may be our last on the planetary plane.

When I ring the doorbell, the boy with the laser gun greets us, and Kate toddles off with him, disappearing into the back rooms. The five pairs of wooden shoes are in the doorway. The cookies are on the table. I can't help but wonder if I'm in a time warp. Wanda sits in the center of the sofa, surrounded by her followers. I know I have seen these people before, yet they all look strange to me. They have bright, bug-eyed stares that make me wonder if they aren't all on drugs.

We wait for a few more people, but no one dares eat a cookie. We remember what happened once before. When we are assembled, Wanda begins to speak. "Because the end is at hand, we need to prepare ourselves. If the predictions are right, we could be called any day. In fact, Ashtar will not be with us tonight. He is busy with preparations. He says to let you know that you, his light workers, may be called at any moment."

There is a tittering in the small group; a palpable excitement passes among us. Wanda smiles, glad to see that we are ready to follow her. "Ashtar has informed me that you should make preparations to depart. Whatever loose ends you need to tie up—debts you owe, matters that only you can attend to—it is important that you put them all in order."

Wanda now seems like a doctor, pronouncing our final illness. The others appear to be focused on matters they need to put in order, but I am more fixated on the word "depart."

Carl, who was at Wanda's house when the earth-based unit was formed, asks if he should sell his car to his brother. A woman named Melanie asks about her children and is reassured that children will accompany their parents.

I raise my hand. "Depart how?" I ask Wanda.

She looks straight at me. "That is being decided."

"But I'd like to know," I say, "so I can plan."

Wanda glares at me now. Her eyes are steely, cold. "You will know when it is decided," she says firmly, "and not before."

After the meeting, we drive down to the cliffs near our house. It is a warm night, and there is a slip of a moon over the Pacific. I park and carry Kate, who is getting sleepy, down to the path. Black water laps the shore below. Seals bark on the rocks offshore. Almost a year ago, when I arrived, I thought about jumping from these cliffs. I came all the way to the edge, and now I am ready to turn around. Now, suddenly, I am thinking about going home.

The New Age

Fifty-three

On May 10, the day when the earth is supposed to end, I am scheduled to have a breast exam. I drive out to a clinic, where they put me in front of a hand-cranked Moviola that shows a woman examining her breasts. As I turn the handle, a dishwater blonde with an expressionless face touches her breasts in a circular motion. I wonder who this woman is. A nurse, maybe. An actress, a former porn queen. What would make her do such a thing?

Afterward they introduce me to Betsi, a strange rubber model. They have me palpitate her breasts, looking for lumps. I do very well, and they give me a high score. This feels a little like a driver's exam of the body, I tell the clinic assistant, but she does not laugh.

On the way home I drive along Canyon Road. It is a beautiful morning, and the fragrance of strawberries is in the air. With my windows down, I can smell them. Strawberry pickers are stooped over in the fields, swaying side by side like elephants in a circus, like palmettos in the breeze. I stop and watch. Their faces are filled with strain and fatigue. I get out of my car, and the whole world smells like ripe strawberries. Going to the shack where they sell them, I buy three pints. They are incredible, delicious, the best strawberries I've ever eaten. I sit on the grassy knoll, staring across the fields, eating them.

Ralph's VW is on this road, and I think I may as well stop and have him look at the windshield wiper one more time. He is there, as is his son. The boy is taking apart an old battery. Ralph waves, a big smile on his face, when he sees me. "I was going to call you," Ralph says. "I've figured out what's wrong."

It's a minor problem, a defect in the socket in which the wiper sits. Ralph has ordered the part, which he now holds up. I help his son with the battery, as Ralph replaces the socket, doesn't charge me. "It won't happen again," Ralph says. "Now you can go anywhere."

I get into the car, make the difficult turn easily now onto the Canyon Road, and head home.

That night Jeremy calls. I hear his voice on the machine, plaintive, begging. "Mary," he says, "this whole thing is a misunderstanding. Please, I need to talk to you."

When I do not pick up, he talks for almost a full hour into my machine—a long discourse about his love for me, how Sigrid doesn't really matter, how his tennis game has improved, how he's leaving for India soon, how he wants to see me in June.

As he rambles on, I glance at the calendar on the wall and remember that today the world was supposed to end. But it didn't. The next day one of the light workers calls and tells me the earthquake happened yesterday as predicted. "Did you feel it?" she asks. I tell her no, and she sounds disappointed. She explains that it was only for the most sensitive of light workers to feel. It was an earthquake of the mind, and everything realigned. The earth reorganized itself at the core. Nostradamus is our lady, and she represents the merging of all female and male principles, and yesterday those principles merged. Today, she says, the New Age has truly begun.

Fifty-four

The American Booksellers Convention comes to Anaheim, and I get a pass from my publisher. Wandering around, I run into my agent at the Disneyland Hotel. Hesitantly she asks about my novel *The Waiting Room,* which I've been working on for so many years. "Oh, it's finished, but it's no good. It's in the drawer."

"You let me be the judge of that," she says. I shrug. "Drop it in the mail," she tells me, exacting a promise.

The following week, still despondent, I drop it in the mail.

Afterward I chase Kate around the living room. We've made up a game called I'm Gonna Get You. I crawl around and say, "I'm gonna get you," and she tries to crawl away, but eventually, of course, I get her, and then she laughs very, very loud. We can play this game for hours. I love to hear her laugh when I get her. It makes me laugh too.

That week I have dinner with Valentine. I tell him that once again I am homesick and broke and don't know how I'll make it through another year. Valentine is not so patient with me this time. He tells me I should smoke marijuana, as he does to calm himself. I tell him that what will calm me is help, money, and someone to love me.

He tells me I'm too stressed out, I worry too much. "You don't know what your assets are. You have your gift," he tells me. "You have your art. And you have your daughter. All this actually makes you more attractive and appealing."

I'm so tired I can barely lift my head, but I listen to what he has to say. "That is what will get you through."

"So cut the crap," he tells me. "And quit feeling sorry for yourself."

A few weeks later I walk with Willa along the beach. Kate toddles behind us, as I tell my friend, "I have my work, my daughter, and my life." I tell her I believe this is enough, that I don't need anything more.

But the next day a note from Jeremy arrives in the mail. I tremble as I open it, afraid of what might be inside. I expect a long, plaintive letter, but instead I find a brief note and a check for a thousand dollars. I stare at this check for quite a while. I need the money desperately. It could tide me over for the summer. It could be my ticket home. I think of all the things I could use it for. But there are some things I cannot compromise, and my daughter is one of them. It's true—isn't it?—that mothers have lifted automobiles off their children. That there are reserves of strength we don't even know we have until they are tested.

I look at this check and long to take it down to my bank in Boat Canyon and fill out a surfer deposit slip and let it buy the time and food and clothes I need. Instead I pick up a pen and write "Void" across it. Then I go to a store and Xerox the check for my records, in case I ever have to prove that I never took a penny from him. And then I put the voided check in an envelope and send it back.

When my agent calls, Kate is in the garden, stuffing her thumbs into the shells of snails. I tap at the window, trying to distract her, as the agent says she loves the new novel, the one I kept in the drawer all those months. As she goes on, Kate sticks her fingers into more snail shells, goo running down her arms. Don't put it in your mouth, I say silently, please don't put it in your mouth. My agent pays me what she says is an agent's highest compliment, which I am barely able to listen to as I tap discreetly on the glass, shaking my head *no no*.

"I read it as if I weren't representing it," I hear her say.

As soon as I am off the phone, I race out to the garden, scoop Kate into my arms. The green goo of dead snails drips down her arms. "This is it!" I tell my daughter as I whirl her around. She laughs gleefully in my arms. "This is good news!" In a week my agent sells the novel for more money than I've ever seen before, enough to tide us over for a while.

I make the decision to leave California and quit my job. I know I can't drive all the way across the country with Kate and our things in the car. Yet the thought of driving cross-country alone intrigues me. I'll have Ramona fly to Chicago with Kate. I get some maps of the West and pick a route. From California to Utah, then up north along 89, then head through Yellowstone and Cody, over to South Dakota, where my friend Dan O'Brien has a ranch. I'll stop there for a few days.

The thought of traveling again enlivens me. It seems that by the summer's end I'll be heading home.

When I inform Jeremy that I won't be seeing him again, he says he wants to be able to see Kate. I think about this for several days. Perhaps I could have lived with the lies, the broken plans, the endless phone calls that led nowhere, but what about Kate? Could she live with canceled visits, missed birthdays? If she is to have a father, I want it to be one she can rely upon.

I call a friend in New York, who puts me in touch with a lawyer, Arthur Canton, and I ask him to draw up two documents. "Nothing fancy, Arthur," I tell him. Arthur knows I can't afford much, so he provides two straightforward letters. One in which Jeremy agrees to acknowledge his paternity, agrees to child support (terms to be negotiated), and regular visitation (terms to be negotiated). In the second document he agrees to relinquish his paternal rights.

When I send him these two documents, Jeremy calls me, irate. "Just what do you mean by this?" he asks, his voice trembling. Since he is rarely angry and almost never raises his voice, I know this has made him very mad. "Just what are your intentions here?"

"They are legal documents," I tell him. "Surely you know how to read them." But I spell it out. I explain that he will either be her father or he will not be her father, but he will not be something in between.

"And if I don't sign either . . . ?"

"Then I will sue you for paternity," I tell him.

"You can't be serious. . . ."

"I have never been more serious," I assure him, and now he knows I mean it. "I don't care what you sign, but sign one of them."

In truth, I do care. I know which one I want to come back to me, and I pray that Jeremy will do the right thing. Finally, a few weeks later, he does. He returns to me his paternal release, relinquishing all claim to Kate. I have no room in my heart to be sentimental about this. I am sad, I am sorry, and I am deeply relieved.

This document will be placed in a vault for the next three years. When Kate is eighteen months old, I meet Larry at a conference. I tell him that my life is complicated and he says it's all right; we can just be friends. We go to films, share books, laugh at the same jokes. He never once refuses a midnight diaper run;

never once says, "It's your kid." We are married the following year. Just before Kate's fourth birthday we will all raise our right hands and a judge in Surrogate Court will declare that Larry is free and clear to adopt her under the laws of the State of New York.

Fifty-five

I'm getting to know the road to Yosemite like the back of my hand. I know the rise through Summit, the turnoff north into the Sierra. I like the names of things. Desert Dynamic, Last Chance Café, Cactus Flats, Mexican Bandit Slope, Desert Mirage (Live Music Every Friday Night), High Desert Casino. I pass Owens Lake, which is little more than a pink alkali flat. And the valley that was drained to provide Los Angeles with its water. The Manzanar Relocation Center stands as a monument to the Japanese detained here during the war.

As we have in the past, Kate and I stop at the Olicante Ranchhouse for the cowboy breakfast. We push on to Mono Lake, to visit Patricia Holland. "I want you to see where we live before you leave California," she said, inviting me.

It is dusk as we pull up to the house. Prehistoric Mono Lake, with its tufa, is filled with brine shrimp, brine flies. Patricia's wood-frame house sits at the foot of the sierra. Her lawn seems to be an endless sprinkler system, watering the burned-out grass. The sun is setting over Mono, and the clouds are a brilliant pink. A wild wind blows from the sierra down to the lake.

There's a party going on when we get there. Sixties music is playing. Women in flouncy skirts and tie-dyed shirts, men in jeans and plaid flannel shirts, sit around, sipping beers. It's potluck, but Patricia told me to just bring beer. I've got some warm six-packs in the trunk, which go right into the fridge.

Patricia greets us with her son, Jake, and her husband, Joe, who will stay only a day, then head back to Los Angeles, where he works in construction. We sit around the table with their friends, have a rice-and-beans dinner, a quiet talk, which gets slightly heated when it turns to the big environmental issue up here. It seems there is talk of drawing water from Mono Lake for Los Angeles. People are angry about this prospect.

The guests leave early. They work early jobs, have kids to get home. Just as the sun is setting, Patricia and I take a walk along the edge of the lake. There is a full moon rising. Tufas stand like odd sentinels. Creatures from another planet, another time. Faces seem to peer out of them like Chinese jade.

In the morning we head to Tuolomne Meadows in Yosemite, where we hike all day, our kids in backpacks. We pause in the meadows to chase mountain bluebirds, butterflies. We eat turkey sandwiches and sip bottled water. Then, in the late afternoon, we drive over to June Lake.

It's an Ansel Adams picture: the glacial lake, the tree-lined slopes rising above it. I stick my toe in the lake. It is so cold I think I'll freeze. But Patricia dives in, and even with her bad arm, she does a smooth, steady stroke. Kate and Jake are playing on the shore, digging in the sand. I take them each by the hand, leading them into the water. I am amazed at the numbing chill. The children are stunned as well, but soon they are splashing, getting each other wet, shrieking with joy.

Patricia waves at me to follow, pointing at the lifeguard seated on a chair nearby. The guard gives me a nod, saying he'll watch the kids. I give Kate a kiss, telling her to be good. First I get my legs wet, then my thighs. The icy water rises to my waist, tingles around my breasts. At last I dive.

The water is dark, almost black, and freezing cold. Numbness races through my limbs, then my body feels zapped, revived. I swim out, following Patricia into the center of the lake. We swim until we float on our backs, waving at the children, who wave back at us from the shore.

Fifty-six

Every summer in Laguna, there is the Starfair, the Laguna Beach Visionary Arts expo, whose motto is "The last frontier is the space between us." I am packing now, shipping twenty-four cartons of books home. Then I will pack the car with my computer, what possessions I do not mail, and drive home, while Kate flies to my parents' with Ramona.

When Willa arrives, she sees me sorting out books, folding clothes that Kate's outgrown. "You can't leave Laguna and not attend the Starfair." She has tickets for Friday night.

Together we wander among the airbrushed visionary oil paintings, admire the work of Remlow Blevins, maker of aquatic sculptures—"The Resurrection," "Ode to a Shell," "The Temptation of Sand," fashioned of carved foam, poured plastic, cut glass, strobe lights.

That evening we attend the *tableaux vivants*. This is the grand spectacle that participants prepare for all summer. People pose as works of art. I sit in the audience, watching *Un Dimanche à la Grande Jatte,* a painting by Seurat I have admired for years in the Art Institute of Chicago. The curtain pulls back, and there, after months of preparation, is, frozen in time for five minutes, *La Grande Jatte.* No Jackson Pollack here.

It is followed by *The Perfect Wave:* a silver wave with a silver surfer, perfectly poised, motionless. As his platform slowly turns, the surfer perches at the crest, just before the wave crashes on his head. And there, for an instant, I see my life, frozen, poised, as I am about to move on.

As we leave the Starfair, I pause to have my aura photographed. The aura reader uses a special light, asks me to stand perfectly still, then takes a Polaroid. A few moments later she hands me a print. It shows a dozen or so dark circles with bright halos around them, like total eclipses of the sun. Or like something you don't want to find under a microscope. The aura reader explains that I am truly a creature of light. Pure energy of a mental nature. The light, she assures me, shines through here.

Acknowledgments

With special thanks to Bill Bremer, for the safety of his bungalow, his walks with Kate, and his information on superstition; Chris Merrill, who spoke to me about fundamentalism; Kaaren Kitchell; and Mary Jane Roberts, my port in the storm, my companion on some of these outings; Annie Glenn, Vicky Elliot, Peter Allen, who shared his knowledge of Jung and Buddhism with me; to knowledgeable friends Bill Selby, David Ravel, and Sean MacCracken; to Irvine and San Francisco friends, especially Oakley Hall, who was a friend when I needed one, and everyone at Squaw, and dear Sylvia Easton, whom I will always remember, and Dave Easton, who opened their hearts and were family to us. With thanks to Ellen Levine and her agency and to Diane Higgins at Picador for all their support; to my research assistant, Brooke deBlois, and to Julie and Ruebiger J. Flik for a summer travel grant, awarded through Sarah Lawrence College. To my parents for all their support over the years. To blessed readers Larry O'Connor and Dani Shapiro, and to beloved daughter, Kate.

Yours in cosmic love

About the Author

Mary Morris is the author of ten books: four novels, three collections of short stories, and three travel memoirs, including *Angels & Aliens.* She has also coedited with her husband, Larry O'Connor, *Maiden Voyages,* an anthology of the travel literature of women. Her numerous short stories and travel essays have appeared in such publications as *The Paris Review, Vogue,* and *The New York Times.* The recepient of the Rome Prize in Literature and a Guggenheim fellowship, Morris teaches creative writing at Sarah Lawrence College and lives in Brooklyn with her husband and daughter.